MW00981721

## MAXIMUM RETURN
## WINNER
## BENJAMIN FRANKLIN AWARD
## BEST BUSINESS BOOK

Maximum Return is excellent. I am in sales and use the book to help me develop business cases for customers. The book is easy to understand and follow. Congratulations on winning the Benjamin Franklin Award for best business book. I can see why you won!

> T, Nantz
> AVP Sales, Integrated Access

Patrick Gregory's down-to-earth style speaks to the realities of managing the capital approval process in the business world. His advice is sound, extremely thorough and accessible to anyone in the organization.

> Christopher P. Johns
> Vice President & Controller, PG&E Corporation

It's natural for project managers and sponsors to overstate a project's financial merit. Maximum Return is the reality check all companies need to ensure that objectives, assumptions, and commitments are both realistic and obtainable.

> William H. Schaefer, P.E.
> Manager of Business Development,
> GTE Telecommunication Services, Inc.

This book is exactly what project managers need in order to develop more credible financial projections.

> N. David Bruce
> U.S. Controller & Principal, Barclays Global Investors

*About the Benjamin Franklin Award:*
Named in honor of America's most cherished publisher/printer, the Publishers Marketing Association's Benjamin Franklin Award recognizes excellence in independent publishing. Publications, grouped by genre, are judged on editorial and design merit by top practitioners in each field. Judges come from all areas of the industry: major newspaper publishers, artists and business writers who serve the industry. The Awards were presented in New York City, where winners were recognized for setting the standards and pace for the publishing industry.

# MAXIMUM RETURN

# MAXIMUM RETURN

## PATRICK J. GREGORY

LIVING SPIRT PRESS

Maximum Return
© Copyright 2003 by Patrick J. Gregory

Library of Congress Catalog Card Number 2002092526
ISBN 0-9672776-3-9

Book designed by Michael Saint James
Cartoon illustrations by Dean Roberts
Original cover art created by Neil Osborn

All rights reserved. No part of this book may be reproduced
or transmitted in any form or by any means, electronic or
mechanical, including photocopying, recording, or by any
information storage and retrieval system, without
permission in writing from the author.

Published by
Living Spirit Press
P.O. Box 2455
Walnut Creek, CA 94595
www.maximumreturn.net

*To Ann and Kalen — the maximum
return in my life.*

# ACKNOWLEDGMENTS

As I'm sure other authors can relate to, the writing of this book took considerably more time and effort than I initially anticipated. Throughout it all, I wish to acknowledge the unwavering support that my wife, Ann, has given me. I am forever grateful especially for the many sacrifices that she and my daughter, Kalen, have made.

I am also very grateful to Tom Gregory for his insightful and creative editorial reviews and helpful business advice. A special thanks also goes to Dean Roberts who provided the fantastic drawings that can be seen throughout the book. Dean's wonderful artwork helped to turn what is traditionally a dull subject into something fun to read.

I would also like to acknowledge the following people who reviewed the early manuscripts and provided outstanding feedback: David Bruce, Nancy DeLong-Gregory, Chris Johns, Bill Marshuetz, Tom Partlow, and Stephan Roche. I am thankful to you all for your support and constructive advice. I especially enjoyed the feedback from Nancy DeLong-Gregory who I feel was a good representative for those individuals in the corporate world who consider themselves to be less than "financially savvy." Nancy feels that the book addresses a critical business need for the many workers outside of Finance who are involved with project spending. She believes that because of this book, groups outside (and inside) of the Finance organization will now stand a better chance at making more enlightened decisions. Nancy was also surprised at how a book on this subject could be so enjoyable, and she even found the financial analysis chapter to be written in manner that was easy to understand (and would not put her to sleep!)

Thanks also goes to Christine Mattsson for her cheerleading during the project's formative stages and to Bill Schaefer for his support. And thanks to JD for the inspiration.

On the production end, special thanks to Neil Osborn (cover artist) and Michael Saint James of Citron Bay Press. Michael's creativeness in book design brings life to some pretty "creatively-challenging" subject matter. It has been a pleasure working with him.

And finally, I am grateful for the assistance of Rich Gray. I deeply appreciate Rich's dedication, enthusiasm and support on this project. He was always there to encourage me, and I value our friendship greatly.

# TABLE OF CONTENTS

**6. Financial Analysis – Show Me the Money (continued)**

# PREFACE

What you are about to read was developed over the course of ten years of hands-on operating experience and represents my attempt at addressing a serious problem faced by many companies. During that time I have held numerous financial management positions in several different industries including the automotive, aerospace, utility and financial services industries. What finally motivated me to start writing was the lousy job my company (who I no longer work for and who shall remain nameless) was doing in analyzing, approving and managing capital projects. It seemed that most people in the company could care less about the capital investment-side of the business. The company had no effective process to follow, and there was also no financial incentive to make people care. Sure, there were operating budgets that people had to meet, and their pay was duly affected, but capital budgets (the pots of money used for funding long-term investments) were never closely managed. Frustrated and concerned over my company's situation, I decided to investigate what other companies were doing. To my surprise, the research revealed that my company's situation was not unique by any means.

Now, you might be asking, "Why am I taking this so personal?" "So what if the capital project process is not well managed. Welcome to the world of big companies!" Well, it did matter to me because it was my responsibility to let management know if they were spending the company's money wisely. I found myself faced with two choices:

◇ I could either continue with the present process of whoever yelled the loudest or knew the right people got the money, or

◇ I could develop a better and more disciplined approach that tried to minimize office politics.

I realized that in order for a better process to succeed, it would have to be developed keeping the interests of the operating areas in mind. Since I had worked closely with operations people (the ones who typically offered up new project ideas), I knew that I had to lose my "finance hat" and use non-financial jargon, or the material would fall on deaf ears. And I would have to design something that would be different than what was taught in schools, which typically just focused on financial analysis. I also wanted a process that expanded the traditional concept of financial return to one that incorporated non-financial returns as well. Although the financial return was important, it is often the non-financial parts of a project that determine whether the project succeeds or fails. Just paying attention to whether a project was financially justifiable seemed myopic. Finally, if a new process was going to work, the paperwork processing had to be as simple and straightforward as possible. Although you would like to think otherwise, when it comes to filling out forms for some corporate requirement, such as project justification, most operating people want to be told what to do. But most companies do a very poor job communicating these requirements and, more importantly, in giving their employees the tools and training to conduct a proper project analysis.

*Maximum Return* offers a complete step-by-step approach for analyzing project decisions. This book focuses heavily on the "people side" of the process, and it is a relatively easy read for those who have little or no financial background. Non-financial people will truly welcome the "user-friendly" advice on how to prepare a quality financial analysis and project business case. This book will appeal to the finance community too. Finance personnel will want to read it so they can gain a greater appreciation of how to improve their working relationships with their clients.

Capital project budgets in many companies are often quite large and for a good reason. These projects lay the foundation for a company's future. If your company is struggling with how to effectively manage this process, then the highly practical recommendations included in this book will be of great value. And even if you feel your situation is unique, you will see that this book's guidance is adaptable to just about any type of project or business environment—be it big or small, complex or simple. Be sure your project teams read this book *before* they spend your company's money!

– Patrick J. Gregory

---

The author will be happy to discuss how this book can be adapted or re-designed to meet the specific needs of your company. Please contact him at:

The Stonehaven Group
P.O. Box 2455
Walnut Creek, CA 94595
(925) 256-0335

Contact information can always change. Check our website for the most current information.

www.maximumreturn.net
patrickgregory@maximumreturn.net

# THE CAPITAL PROJECT CHALLENGE

Y ou have a great idea for a project. One that has "success" written all over it. One that will certainly position you well for that big promotion. Putting together a project proposal or business case in order to get the project approved seems like a rather straight forward task, but your past experience tells you otherwise. "If only those bean counters would let us focus on things that really make money for the company instead of this paperwork" you grumble.

Twenty floors up in the executive washroom a senior manager who is responsible for reviewing next year's capital budget laments to a fellow manager, "This Company has a tradition of coming up with lots of ideas for projects that promise great value but never fully deliver. The stack of proposals on my desk all promise high returns, but it's impossible to tell which ones are truly sound business investments. If the sponsors say these projects will generate high returns, then we should hold them accountable for the results!"

Management often believes that the major problem with projects lies not so much with the approval process (because they are normally involved) but with people not delivering what they promised. Moreover, management is convinced that more controls are needed to manage the situation and improve performance. However, the question that management fails to consider is: "What is the real cause behind poor project performance?"

While it certainly may be true that some projects are well thought-out and fail because of implementation mistakes, many if not most fail because of poor up-front planning. Even the best workers in the world will have difficulty implementing a poorly designed plan. The purpose of this book is to provide practical guidance on how to improve the most critical phase in a project's life cycle—the planning process. Specifically, the focus is on improving the **process** for evaluating and preparing the business cases of major capital projects. A business case is the defining document for a project. It lays out the project's strategy, provides justification for access to funding, and becomes a blueprint for beginning work on a project. It is also a critical element of many companies' capital budgeting processes.

## WARNING SIGNS

As anyone familiar with building construction will tell you, a sound set of blueprints is the first requirement for constructing a stable structure. Problems that arise in this stage of development could have serious consequences on the ultimate success of the project. Don't wait for project after project to fail in your company before you decide to take action. Be on the look out for any of the following signs that your company may have a weak planning process:

- ❖ Lack of accountability – projects seem to have a life of their own; and it's often difficult to determine who was responsible when a project fails to deliver

- ❖ Lack of teamwork – the project involved many cross-organizational commitments of personnel and resources that were not delivered on time. Everyone bought off on the plan when the project was approved; when resources were needed, the project all of a sudden had low priority

- ❖ Projects not completed on time – what originally was promised to be finished in a matter of months now stretched into years; project requirements continually change

✧ Spending over budget – the original justification grossly underestimated the project's expenses; large sections of the project were mistakenly left out of the business case

✧ Benefits not realized – the project failed to return promised benefits; projections were too optimistic or unrealistic, and calculating the actual benefits the company would realize was nearly impossible

✧ Non-standard project proposals – business cases were not developed in a consistent manner thereby making it difficult to compare projects; proper authorization was not acquired before work on the project was started

**1**

## CREATING THE VISION

Managing the capital spending process within a company is a challenging task. The project problems described above usually begin within one operating area, but they ultimately impact the performance of the entire company. Because of this, it becomes senior management's responsibility to take corrective action. A process must be created and managed that will ensure that:

✧ Accountability is designed into the approval process. Accountability is no longer something that should be determined *after* problems develop and the big money is spent.

✧ Cross-functional commitments are properly prioritized and agreed upon in writing. No longer will departments say they were not aware of projects.

✧ Realistic time lines are presented along with an open discussion of what can go wrong with the project.

✧ Realistic cost assumptions are developed and adhered to. Standardized cost checklists will be followed to ensure that the project accounts for all costs.

✧ Realistic benefit assumptions are developed and tested for attainability. The quality of the assumptions is assessed and the issue of verifying the results is discussed in the business case.

✧ A standardized business case template is adopted thereby making it easier to compare projects. No longer will management struggle with the operations' "creativeness" in their project proposals, and no longer will the project teams have to guess at what management wants to see.

To read more about the challenges companies face in managing this process read **Why Project Approval is so Challenging** and **Business Case Development – The Myth & The Reality** in the Appendix.

## "I Can't Take It Any More" – A Personal Challenge

As many of you can personally attest to, a poorly designed process can wreak havoc on an organization. The frustration is usually first felt where the ideas for projects are born. Operations personnel easily become annoyed and over-whelmed by the never-ending stream of bureau-cratic demands. To them, the goal is to produce projects that generate revenue, not paperwork. From a headquarters' view, corporate managers are mystified by the operations' failure to comply with the rules. Nobody seems to analyze projects in a consistent manner. The financial documentation is often incom-plete or weak at best, and seldom is there a good discussion on whether the project meets the strategic needs of the company. The rules are there to help them, management may say, and the operations' behav-ior could be considered insubordinate.

This sense of frustration experienced by management was eloquently captured in a memorandum from the Group Controller of a major aerospace corporation to the senior management within that group. In the memo, the Controller expressed management's concerns over the seemingly ad-hoc nature of its project approval process. (It's a long memo, but well worth the read!)

---

To:        Division Managers

Subject:   Appropriations Requests and Program Letters

Sorry I haven't responded sooner to your recent memo requesting guidance on appropriation requests (AR). With respect to a "model" AR, I'd suggest you talk to the Systems Operation Division about the AR and preliminary presentations they put together for their new facility. The financial data were complete and reasonably well presented, and the text was pretty much to the point.

It would be a mistake, though, to try to simply copy their format or transpose their financial schedules to your division or anywhere else. The point is, their package was complete and well thought out. It answered all the important questions and required only

---

1

minor (and few) requests for additional data or clarifications.

While your memo addressed only ARs, the same concerns apply to program letters, advance requests, etc. Quite frankly, in my experience, nobody in the Corporation does a consistently good job on any of these. As we discussed briefly at a recent group finance meeting, recurring "sins" in this area generally fall into the following categories:

- Committee Syndrome: Letters are the collective product of several authors and display obvious "cut-and-paste" efforts. As a result, continuity suffers, logic is obscure, and emphasis and priorities are inappropriate. A remedy is simply discipline and willingness to do a final rewrite, rather than a patch-job.

- Stream of Consciousness Approach: Text starts from the basics and laboriously builds to a conclusion (or request for something). By the time the reader gets to the conclusion, he's lost, tired or frustrated. Again, a rewrite's a solution; start with the conclusion, then fill in the "how's" and "why's."

- Incompleteness: There are many manifestations of this, including omission of key material, failure to state not only the "what" but also the "why," failure to explicitly draw the conclusion (which may be obvious to the writer, but possibly not to the reader), faulty or partially-sound logic, etc. The solution is more discipline on the writer's part.

- Superfluity and the "Tonnage" Syndrome: Inclusion of irrelevant data, either because it shows how smart the writer is or because it pads out the document. The solution is simply to edit it out—again, requiring discipline and effort.

- Undisciplined Financial Data: Including incompleteness, superfluity, redundancy, lack of tie-points to text or other exhibits, poor layout, illogical flow, etc. One more time: discipline is required.

- Failure to Meet Submission Deadlines: Sometimes the stock excuses are valid, but not that often.

- Package not Self-Contained (related to "Incompleteness"): The package assumes prior knowledge on the reader's part for key elements necessary to a full understanding of the issues. Sometimes this is done via reference to a previous presentation or document.  Generally speaking, the reader is not going to have time to find the prior reference.  The solution is to summarize within the present package salient points of the reference.  The test of "self-containedness" is whether or not an intelligent, but relatively uniformed, reader (the proverbial man from Mars) would understand the key issues from reading the package itself.  Alternatively, imagine reading it yourself a year from now: would it be fully understandable?

In summary, improvement in these areas requires work, education, and consistent, day-to-day follow-up.  It won't just happen.  You might note, I have not mentioned poor English as a major problem – poor writing is, in the sense of illogical thinking and construction of the argument.

I realize most of our ARs and approval letters originally are drafted by technical people who may not be able to see their subject from a "management" standpoint.  But, "management" is the approver, so an emulsifier is required to join together technical oil and management water.  Traditionally, and also by formal assignment, Finance is charged with the emulsifier role.  Therefore, it's up to us to cast approval requests in terms that are meaningful to "management."  The closer we can come to this at the operations' level, the easier and faster will approvals be effected.

Finally, all approval requests have a substantial salesmanship element – just as contract proposals do – which should not be overlooked.  By this I don't mean that facts should be slanted, but neither is it incumbent on us to cite irrelevant detractions.  And attention should be paid to "setting up the duck, then knocking it down" – e.g., citing a risk and then explaining how we've minimized it.  (Too frequently, we only set it up.)

We are experiencing continuing problems with approvals, particularly those at the Corporate Staff level.  Unless we can improve our collective performance in this area, our group's relationship with the Corporation will suffer.  Consequently, achievement of our business objectives may be compromised.  To avoid this, we need to continue to work on this problem group-wide, and to this end we'll continue to address it within Finance at our periodic meetings.

Group Controller

## MAXIMUM RETURN...

✓ Offers comprehensive and standardized business case templates complete with user-friendly instructions

✓ Guides the user in preparing a quality business analysis of the proposed project

✓ Provides easy-to-understand advice on how to prepare a sound financial justification

✓ Examines risks associated with the project

✓ Reviews the "people" elements (within and outside the project team) that are needed to make the project successful

✓ Presents the business case in a format that management will greatly appreciate

✓ Will help create a more disciplined and thorough capital project review process within your company

## THE SOLUTION

*Maximum Return* directly addresses the "recurring sins" mentioned by the Group Controller. This book defines an approach for business case development that will significantly reduce the frustration experienced within your company.

At the heart of this book is a comprehensive set of templates and instructions designed specifically for project teams. Written in mostly non-financial language, project managers (and the individuals "volunteered" to prepare the business cases) will appreciate the step-by-step guidance on how to conduct a thorough business analysis of the proposed project. This analysis is essential not only to convince management that the idea is a good one but also to validate for the project team (and sponsor) that the project is a good strategic fit for the company. Getting the project team more involved in the approval process ultimately strengthens the team's buy-in to the project's commitments and helps to lower implementation risk.

Preparing a quality financial analysis remains the most critical part of the business case because, in most cases, the project will not get approved if it doesn't meet the company's approval criteria for acceptable financial performance. The book's instructions for doing a financial analysis assume that the user has little or no financial background. Obviously, there will be areas where greater financial expertise is required, but not to worry. The book will tell you when you need to seek assistance and from whom to get it. People with limited financial backgrounds will also want to review the additional financial sections in the Appendix. These sections provide greater detail (again, in easier to read language) of the financial analysis concepts used to evaluate the proposal. It is well worth your while to read these sections if you would like to gain a greater appreciation of one of the most important parts in the business case. The book also takes the reader through a thorough review of the risk inherent in the project by asking a series of "What can go wrong?" questions. The goal of this section is not to produce a quantitative analysis but rather a qualitative evaluation of the project's risk profile.

## THERE'S MORE TO "RETURN" THAN JUST MONEY

Even though this book is titled *Maximum Return,* it stresses that returns are not just limited to *financial* returns. They include many *non-financial* elements as well. The book greatly emphasizes the people-side of project planning such as doing an organizational impact analysis and a project team member analysis. These activities all contribute to yielding greater non-financial returns such as improved teamwork, better communication and higher morale. Although difficult to quantify, they are generally acknowledged to lead to greater efficiency and more profits for the company in the medium and long term.

The end result of following this book's approach is the creation of a professional business case that will enjoy a far smoother ride toward approval and eventual success in implementation. It is important to keep in mind that improving the administrative, record-keeping part of project planning is not the primary purpose for installing a more disciplined process—although that is a welcomed benefit greatly appreciated by those charged with such duties. The primary goal is to produce a process that actually yields higher-quality project proposals with significantly lower risk profiles. These

> The primary goal is to produce a process
> that yields higher-quality project proposals
> with significantly lower risk profiles.

lower-risk profiles will better position each new project idea for a successful launch as the project enters its implementation phase. And once projects enter the implementation phase, management will be very interested in tracking their performance. Meaningful project tracking will be all but impossible unless standardized business cases are prepared.

## OVERVIEW OF WHAT'S AHEAD

Before getting into the details of building a business case, let us pause for a moment for a quick overview of how this book is structured. The business case that I recommend you prepare is comprised of seven parts. Each of these parts is covered in a separate chapter in this book and is presented in the same order as would be shown in an actual business case.

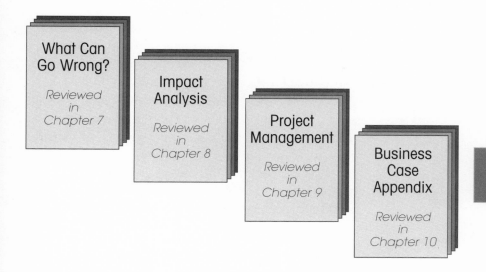

## THE BUSINESS CASE PACKAGE

Each chapter begins with a preview of the template used for that part of the business case and then is followed by detailed instructions on how to complete it. (In some cases, additional templates are interspersed throughout the chapter.) You will find that the recommendations in this book are structured for ease of implementation, and unlike most corporate guidance on this topic, the rationale for each suggestion is also given.

Please note that in some of the chapters you may be asked to consult with others in your company for specific advice, or you may be asked to review some of the concepts presented in the book's Appendix. Completing a business case is something that one individual cannot accomplish in isolation. A quality job requires the input of many people throughout the company. Each chapter will provide direction, at the appropriate stage, on the individuals in your company that you should contact for the needed information.

Before turning to Chapters 4 through 10 to begin work on your business case, please read the two preceding chapters (Chapters 2 and 3). Chapter 2 provides key guiding principles that are fundamental to preparing any business case, and Chapter 3 provides a good preview of the entire business case package. The final chapters (Chapters 11 and 12) offer practical advice on how to get your business case over the seemingly insurmountable hurdle of company politics. All of your work will be for naught unless you can convince management to "sign on the dotted line."

## THE CHALLENGE

You may ask, "How can one offer advice on a subject that appears to be so different—even among companies within the same industry?" Even within the same company, the nature of projects can be so varied that it seems difficult to design a common approach that will work for everyone. Although the complexities among different businesses make this a challenge, there is a set of core practices or processes that are indeed shared by all.

At a conceptual level, all of the information presented in this book revolves around:

✧ Technique

✧ Product

✧ Process

*Technique* refers to the more traditional, analytical way of looking at projects. The focus here is on using the right financial formula. As you might suspect, companies use many techniques, and there is no one right answer. When it comes to financial analysis, using the most complex and sophisticated analytical technique is not always the best approach. Usually a few companies (like those with heavy research and development spending) require them but most do not. *Maximum Return* focuses on using proven, mainstream analytical concepts that will be readily understood by senior management and the project teams.

*Product* refers to the actual packaging of your business case. Organizing your work to convey maximum value to management and the project team is an area where this book excels. The seven-part business case template will work for any kind of project or program.

*Process* refers to the steps you need to take in order to apply the technique, produce the business case, and ready your project for the implementation phase. The steps outlined in each chapter establish a process that can be easily replicated throughout your company. Although your company may be comprised of many different operating entities, there's a lot to be said for using a consistent approach. A standardized process for evaluating major capital spending decisions will greatly assist senior management as it seeks to determine which projects will yield the most value for company shareholders.

## WHO SHOULD READ THIS BOOK

The primary beneficiaries of the advice given in this book are the individuals on the front lines of product development:

✧ The business case preparers

✧ The project managers and their teams

✧ The sponsors (the senior managers of the operating areas that "own" the projects)

But let's be realistic here. Those who have to complete the paperwork will probably always view the project approval process as a "necessary evil"—no matter how well it is improved. At least, by removing the guesswork and gamesmanship from the process, line managers will be able to focus on creating new product ideas instead of trying to determine which format "works" this week.

This book's guidance can also benefit many other functional areas in the organization, and it should be included as part of a mandatory training program for anyone involved in the project approval process—even if that involvement is just limited to *reading* business cases. Senior management, particularly the Chief Financial Officer, the Chief Information Officer and the Controller will find this material essential for establishing policy relating to the management of the capital budgeting and approval process. If your company's controls are weak in this area, this book will provide the necessary guidance that your company's auditors will demand for such an important process.

The emphasis so far has been on projects internal to the company. One can also expand his/her view and examine how this philosophy can impact the company's external clients. Sales people might consider how this guidance could be used for creating business cases for *their* clients. In other words, if your organization requires business cases for major purchases, it is probably safe to assume that your clients have similar requirements for buying your products. By constructing your sales presentations accordingly, you can greatly assist your customers with their buying decisions and consequently generate more sales.

Capital project analysis is a function that usually few can claim as a full-time responsibility. Whether it is leading a new project team or making a large acquisition, at some time or other most everyone will directly experience the process. Instead of acknowledging the importance of capital budgeting and project analysis, most people tend to take a reactive approach—getting involved only when necessary. Capital budgeting is simply too important a matter to not aggressively manage. Just like knowing your company's vision or guiding principles, having a well thought-out process (that is understood by all employees) for examining capital project decisions is fundamental to the future success of your company.

## WHAT THIS BOOK IS NOT ABOUT

This book will not discuss how to manage your project. Instead it will focus on writing a business case that is strategically and financially sound. In the life cycle of a project, this book concentrates on the phases where the project idea is born, the project proposal is developed, and where the project is finally approved.

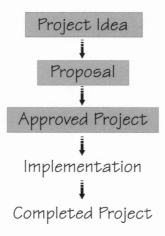

There is no guarantee that by merely following the format shown in this book (or the workbooks) that your project will be approved. Borderline or poor projects will be difficult to approve no matter how well they are packaged. Hopefully this guidance will highlight the weaknesses in such projects and force the project's manager or sponsor to rectify any problems or reconsider submission altogether.

## PUSHING THE ENVELOPE

The importance of how a company manages its capital projects cannot be under estimated. Poor decisions made today can affect earnings for years to come. It is my belief that many projects are born of great ideas but ultimately fall short of expectations principally because of weak planning. A good, solid foundation cannot be laid for a project without a good planning phase that includes the development of a detailed business case. Like trying to build a house on a very poor foundation, if it doesn't collapse while you are putting it up, it will surely be a source of continued trouble in the future.

> "Today's problems came from yesterday's solutions."
> —PETER SENGE

Whether you are a manager in charge of one project or a manager overseeing all of your company's projects, the goal is for you to succeed. As we all know from experience, the correct path to follow is often not the easiest. What this book proposes will be seen by some as requiring more time and effort. If you are pleased with your present process, then go no further. If you picked up this book because you are concerned about your company's capital project planning process, you will not be disappointed with what follows.

❖

# GUIDING PRINCIPLES
# FOR A PRACTICAL APPROACH

D o you believe that people come to work with the best intentions, or do you believe they enjoy looking for ways to make your life difficult? It is my belief that given a choice, most people would prefer to be value-added contributors in their organization. And when it comes to developing business cases for capital projects, most people want to do the right thing. They are frustrated, however, because most companies' processes are poorly structured and offer insufficient guidance. Employees require help in this area, and companies are failing to address their needs. If companies are to improve their capital project review processes, they must take responsibility for providing practical guidance to their employees. This chapter outlines several guiding principles that must be followed in order to have an effective process. It also suggests that an effective process need not be one that is overly complicated. It is strongly recommended that you read this section *before* beginning any work on a business case.

## OPERATING AT THE EXTREMES AND FINDING BALANCE

There is a tendency in the area of managing business case development to operate at the extremes. In one extreme, the business case writer must document every conceivable scenario or permutation of a project. All of these scenarios are evaluated on the company's super computer and monitored by swarms of financial analysts. Direction is very top down, and long lead times are required for project approval. Ford Motor Company is a company that operates close to the extreme.

Ford has been recognized for many years for its strength in the area of financial management, and the company is noted for developing good business acumen within its finance workforce. Project evaluation is a very disciplined process and one that is well incorporated into the company's culture. Financial analysis is extremely detailed, and large financial staffs often expend considerable effort analyzing and re-analyzing projects. Although staffing requirements to support the demands of the process are high, Ford, and many other people as well, believe the benefits far outweigh the costs.

At the other extreme are companies with no formal approaches for project evaluation. Processes are not well defined, and projects are not reviewed in a systematic manner. Decisions are seldom made on the merits of the case but rather on who displays the best advocacy skills. Telling the boss what she wants to hear is often the most effective method for selling your case. Holding people accountable for performance is also just wishful thinking because the process is not disciplined enough to demand adequate documentation. Companies that operate at this extreme tend to focus their efforts on the back end of the process—figuring out what went wrong after the project fails and the big money is spent. Is there another way to manage that doesn't place us at the extremes?

The answer is yes. Just as with many things in our lives, the optimum state is rarely at the extremes. A more balanced approach to business case development focuses on improving the quality of project reviews and how value is delivered to the company. It also eliminates or minimizes the need for post-project autopsies. A balanced approach is not only more desirable but definitely more sustainable in the long run.

## Project Evaluation / Business Case Development

| Have It Your Way | Analysis Overkill |
|---|---|
| Informal Process | Complex, formal process |
| Fast turnaround on decisions | Long lead-time required |
| Basic, incomplete financial analysis | Sophisticated financial analysis |
| Simple analysis tools | State-of-the-art tools |
| Few controls | Tight controls, standards set |
| Reporting formats vary | Standardized, inflexible reporting |
| Limited resources | Resource intensive |
| Additional duty to normal work | Dedicated support staff |
| Inexpensive to maintain | Costly to maintain |

What makes a balanced approach to business case development **balanced**? A balanced approach focuses on the **quality** of the analysis (financial and non-financial) and the **process**. Project teams are encouraged to analyze more than just the usual financial data. In fact, the non-financial analysis is stressed more because this is where most people experience difficulties. By taking a more holistic view, project teams are able to convey to management that they understand…

- ✦ The project's financial impact to the company
- ✦ How it fits with the company's business strategy
- ✦ How it will impact the organizational structure
- ✦ How the company will know if the project is successful once it is completed

A balanced and disciplined approach will ensure that only the most worthy of projects is funded. To move toward a more balanced approach, there are four guiding principles that all project teams (and business-case preparers) must rely on for designing their business cases.

## THE FOUR PRINCIPLES OF PRACTICALITY

All of the advice in this book is guided by four basic Principles of Practicality. These four principles may seem elementary, but it is surprising how often the basics are overlooked.

### 1. KEEP IT SIMPLE

### 2. FOCUS ON PEOPLE AND PROCESS

### 3. PUT IT IN WRITING

### 4. QUANTIFY AND VERIFY YOUR ASSUMPTIONS

> *"I don't exactly know how to describe it, but I'll know it when I see it."*
> — AN ALL-KNOWING SENIOR MANAGER

## 1. Keep it Simple

The things to remember about keeping your business case simple are the following:

✓ Write to the level of the reader

✓ Present a complete picture of the project

✓ Design a good-looking business case package

Simplicity is a relative term. What may seem simple for one person can be highly complex for another. The letter from the controller of the aerospace company (mentioned in Chapter 1) included several references to the need to simplify:

> "...It's up to us to cast approval requests [AR] in terms that are meaningful to management...most of our ARs and approval letters originally are drafted by technical people who may not be able to see their subject from a 'management standpoint'."

The controller's plea is one that is often made but rarely followed. Of course, telling somebody to keep things simple is easier said than done. It does not mean that you have to write everything at a third-grade level, but it does mean that you need to have a heightened awareness of management's likes and dislikes in business cases. You must assess management's level of understanding of your project and prepare your business case accordingly. Talk to people in the group that manages the overall capital spending process (usually the Chief Financial Officer's organization) and discuss senior management's expectations with them.

✓ **WRITE TO THE LEVEL OF THE READER**

---

Writing to the Level of the Reader – A Bad Example

A financial analyst at a large, national company was concerned that its company's financial systems were not optimally configured and that the company's operations were suffering as a result. The analyst repeatedly tried to get a mid-level finance manager to plead his case (to redesign the system) to senior management. The finance manager suggested that the analyst prepare a business case that would document his accusations, discuss the impact to the company and the specific steps needed to affect repair. The analyst agreed.

Instead of receiving a concise, easy-to-follow and well-structured proposal, the manager received a lengthy theoretical paper on how to implement the optimum system configuration. This technical paper was also accompanied by a two-foot by four-foot wide flow chart that diagrammed the proper process flows.

There was absolutely no way that any of the decision-makers would consider reviewing the analyst's "proposal." It would be analogous to taking a car with engine trouble to a mechanic and instead of telling him what we thought was wrong, we would hand him the detailed specifications and drawings of a fully functioning engine. Just telling someone how a good engine (or process) should work does not fix the problem.

It is very easy for technical people (who are often the authors of the business cases) to assume that management can speak the same language and have a good working knowledge of their function. It becomes critically important to develop the ability to distill technical jargon into its basic components. **Unless you are absolutely sure that management is technically proficient, never assume that they will understand.** In the analyst's case, any attempt to convince management to change the financial system was doomed to fail unless the argument could be made using terms the decision-makers could understand.

Another component of simplicity includes presenting a complete picture of the project to your audience. This implies that you know who your audience is and have a good understanding of their knowledge of the project including its history. If you are unsure of your audience's knowledge level, assume they are uninformed. Presenting a complete picture does not mean you have to redo previous work. But it does mean that you should reference it and have it available for review if necessary. Complexity in the process is increased if the reader is forced to do research in order to complete the whole picture.

✓ **PRESENT A COMPLETE PICTURE OF THE PROJECT**

One of the potential side effects of an incomplete business case is that it often takes longer for management to review and approve the case. The author also risks damaging his or her credibility for delivering a less-than-thorough package. Understanding the "bigger picture" provides an all-important context for management to assess how the project under review fits into the company's operating strategy.

There is an old parable that effectively expresses the importance of understanding the bigger picture. I have heard this story used in many different ways but never for business case development. It does seem appropriate, however.

As three blind men encountered an elephant, each exclaimed aloud. "It is a large rough thing, wide and broad, like a rug," said the first, grasping an ear. The second, holding the trunk, said, "I have the real facts. It is a straight and hollow pipe." And the third, holding a front leg, said, "It is mighty and firm, like a pillar."

By not being shown the bigger picture (i.e. having the entire elephant described), management may be blind to the significance of the individual project as it relates to the company's portfolio of projects. Decisions might be made that could impact parts of the organization that were not previously considered.

Another somewhat obvious item that always seems to get overlooked is the simplicity in the design of the business case package. Package design is always a key component in the success of a company's product, and it is no less important in business case development. The final product must be pleasing to the eye and laid out in a straightforward manner. Your goal is to want management to actually look forward to reviewing your proposal. While business cases are inherently not as colorful and entertaining as commercial products, you should strive to create a package that effectively communicates the content. As many people know, poor packaging can doom a great product.

✓ **DESIGN A GOOD-LOOKING BUSINESS CASE PACKAGE**

## 2. FOCUS ON PEOPLE AND PROCESS

Your efforts in developing business cases should focus on people and process and not just numbers. All too often, the typical company business case includes only a few financial spreadsheets and a paragraph or two description of the project. The point is not to downplay

---

Imagine for a moment that you are a project manager...

Think of the names of all the people who will make up your project team. To a large degree, your success (your project's and your own) will be found in your relationships with these people.

 ✧ If your relationships are fruitful, so shall your project bear fruit.
 ✧ If your relationships are troubled, so shall your project be plagued by troubles.

People can become either a source of strength or a source of strife. The choice is up to you.

the importance of having quality financial data, just to highlight that there are other non-financial components of the process that are important too.

Project development is a **team sport**. Like a conductor of a large orchestra, a project manager must carefully direct the movements of many individuals across the organization if he or she is to succeed. If your process just focuses on developing the financial justification, you may be setting yourself up for considerable difficulties in managing the project across the organization once it gets implemented.

**2**

## 3. Put it in Writing

Many of the points discussed in the *Keep it Simple* section touched upon the need for a more effective writing style. *Put it in Writing* is not focused on style but on documentation. One of the recurring sins of business case development is not putting critical information in writing. Examples of inadequate documentation include poorly defined assumptions, incomplete financial analysis and insufficient business justification.

Two of the primary reasons for poor documentation include a lack of discipline in the process and a fear of being held accountable. Without clear guidance and a disciplined process on how to structure a business case, the tendency is for people to select the path that requires the least amount of work. For many people there is also a fear that the more I put in writing, the greater the probability that management will expect me to actually deliver something. The primary benefit of providing written documentation therefore is accountability. As was said earlier, project managers are entrusted with spending the company's money wisely, and it is not too much to ask that they deliver what was promised in the project proposal.

Putting something in writing also sends a very powerful and potentially motivating message to the project team that should not be overlooked. It is not enough to just **think** about how you might do something. It is not enough to just **say** how things should be done either. As we know from personal experience, these are the easy steps. Remember the line, "Talk is cheap"? A **written** confirmation of your intentions will help take you to the next step—which is the implementation or the **"actually doing it"** stage.

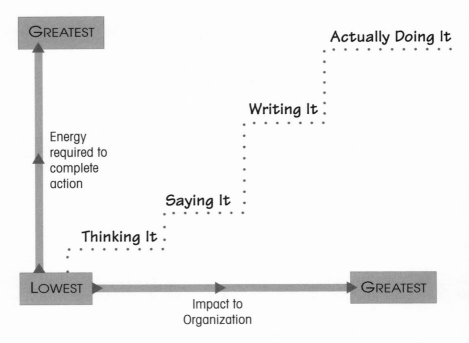

A final benefit of putting it in writing is to provide a historical record for your company. Thorough documentation of your efforts may offer valuable insight and guidance for similar projects your company may undertake in the future. Think of the resources that could be saved if the lessons learned on one project were transferred to subsequent generations of projects.

## 4. QUANTIFY AND VERIFY YOUR ASSUMPTIONS

The first three principles have touched upon various components of effective communication, be it communicating to management or the project team or maintaining a good written record of the project. The final guiding principle involves the financial assumptions and is one that is often violated by those who prepare the financial modeling of a business case. Even though this is the area people tend to focus their energy on, most financial analyses are of questionable quality and often lack a sense of realism. Business cases are considered high quality if the financial assumptions are both *quantifiable* and *verifiable*.

> Quantifiable:  Assumptions are readily measurable.
>
> Verifiable:  Results can be readily measurable.

## QUANTIFIABLE ASSUMPTIONS

Financial assumptions are quantifiable if they are readily measurable. Suppose that your company is buying a software program that promises to greatly improve productivity through improved work processes. You determine that by installing this software program your company could eliminate one department thereby reducing staff by fifteen people and saving the company $3 million. If that assumption is valid, then the benefit will be directly measurable. There is no guesswork required in calculating the savings. There may be a problem on the other hand, if you determined the benefit to be a savings of one-half of one person's work per department for fifty departments throughout the company. Unless your work force is hourly and you can shorten people's workdays, just saying you would improve everyone's productivity is not a good, quantifiable assumption. This would be a difficult assumption to implement although one might counter that these people are now free to do other valuable things for the company. This may be true, but unless those other things bring in extra revenue or reduce costs there is no tangible benefit to the company.

The example given above is typical of the "low-quality" or "soft" assumptions that are often used in business cases. You can include soft assumptions in business cases, just be sure to label them as such. Be careful, however, not to set yourself up by intimating that a soft assumption is "money in the bank." Quantifiable assumptions, whose calculations are straightforward and easy to implement, represent better financial assumptions.

The goal is always to challenge the integrity of the assumptions.

✧ What is the source of the data?

✧ Is it difficult to measure?

✧ Can you visualize that assumption being turned into cash?

Non-Financial Measures: An Example

Often times a project may produce benefits that are difficult to quantify financially. In these cases it is desirable to identify the non-financial measurables that one can use to gauge success.

Suppose, for example, your city has a rapid transit system, and you are the project manager of a proposal that would improve the system's operating performance. According to your proposal, you conservatively estimate that upgrading your system's twenty-year old computer network could increase performance by over 15%. This improvement would directly translate to shortening everyone's commute by 15%. You theorize that this improvement might entice more commuters to give up their cars for mass transit thereby increasing the organization's passenger revenues. *Is revenue a good measure to gauge the success of the project once it is completed? What if revenue only went up 5%? Would the shortfall indicate a problem with the project or somewhere else?*

Increased passenger revenue is clearly an important variable to monitor, but there are many other factors that affect revenues as well, such as the city's economic condition or alternatives to the transit system. Developing non-financial measures is just as important as tracking the financial assumptions. In this example, the business case should include productivity measures that will directly monitor system performance. Once specific metrics (e.g. train transit times) for project performance are developed, one can then proceed to translate them into acceptable financial assumptions.

## VERIFIABLE ASSUMPTIONS

Once you commit to improving performance by 15%, as in the above example, the specific measures that are defined to track perfor-mance can be used to verify the success of the project as it moves forward. Having data assumptions that are verifiable means that the

> Developing non-financial metrics, such as productivity measures, are just as important as tracking financial assumptions.

**2**

source of the data has high integrity, **and** internal processes are in place to measure performance once the project gets underway. If the sources of the assumptions are questionable (i.e. "back-of-the-envelope" approach) then your ability to deliver your project's commitments is at risk.

Another frequently observed weakness in developing business cases is presenting financial assumptions that are not aligned with the way the company records costs and benefits in its accounting system. In the earlier example of a project whose benefit was productivity improvements of one-half person per department for fifty departments, productivity is not an item that is directly measurable in a financial system. Productivity would have to be translated into specific, measurable components before the assumption becomes worthy of consideration.

As you examine a business case, it is important to keep in mind how one would do the "score keeping" after the project gets started. This concern goes back to the issue of accountability. If you are a project manager, how will the company know that you delivered on your cost and benefit assumptions? Who will keep score? How will you know whether you deserve a big bonus or if you should be updating your resume?

While the better cases tend to contain quantifiable and verifiable assumptions, sometimes you might want to include items that are difficult to measure and verify. Again, it is important that such assumptions be labeled as "soft" benefits or costs. You should also thoroughly discuss the merits of each assumption, why it should be included in the business case, and how it creates value for the company.

All things being equal, the more up front and honest you are about the quality of the assumptions used in your business case, the more management will trust you. The goal for developing a quality business case is to design a package that is simple to review and self-contained. It should include well-documented financial and non-financial assumptions, and demonstrate thorough communication across the organization. The remaining part of this book will go into the specifics as to how we accomplish this goal.

❖

*"Fundamental progress has to do with the reinterpretation of basic ideas."*
— ALFRED NORTH WHITEHEAD

# PREVIEWING
# THE BUSINESS CASE

B efore embarking on a trip it usually helps to look at a map to get a sense of the direction you must take and the roads you must travel. A brief overview of the chapters that follow will help orient you to the path ahead. As you will soon discover, preparing a good business case is something one person cannot complete in an afternoon. It requires an in-depth analytical review, excellent communication skills and teamwork. The material in the following chapters will take you through the steps that are necessary to complete your case. It will also alert you to the situations where you need to get other people involved. Once completed, the seven parts of the business case are designed to provide a thorough assessment of the proposed project. The output from these chapters will proactively address most, if not all, of senior management's concerns.

As mentioned in Chapter 1, this book is organized in a fashion that mirrors the finished product. When completed, the business case will include the following components:

Section      Topic

1.   Executive Summary

2.   Business Analysis

3. Financial Analysis

4. What Can Go Wrong? (Sensitivity Analysis)

5. Impact Analysis

6. Project Management

7. Appendix

This may seem like a rather lengthy list, but each of these sections represents an important piece of a complex puzzle. It is up to you to put the pieces together so that management can gain a clear understanding of your project. Preparing the business case will also greatly benefit the project team once the project moves into the implementation phase. Project design and proposal preparation are extremely complex functions, and it should come as no surprise that the formal review of those activities is extensive.

## ASSEMBLING THE BUSINESS CASE PUZZLE

## THE BUSINESS CASE TEMPLATE

As you begin to examine the following chapters, you will see that each begins with a template for a specific section of the business case. The templates serve as outlines for presenting the information that management requires. Each chapter will guide you through the process of completing the template or in some cases, templates.

You may be wondering why templates are even necessary. After all, many companies do not have formal rules for governing the preparation of business cases. One of the benefits of following a structured approach (that utilizes templates) is that it ensures that discipline is instilled in a very strategic function within the company. Absent any guidelines, people will always have different opinions as to what constitutes a quality project review. These different interpretations often lead to major inconsistencies in the analytical techniques used across operating areas, which may lead to the approval of low-quality or higher-risk project ideas.

A standardized approach to project analysis also takes the guesswork out of the process. Most people want direction. "Just tell me what you want and when you want it, and I will provide it to you" is a sentiment repeatedly voiced by operating people. The vast majority of employees want to do the right thing for the company, but they do not like guessing at the requirements. Give your employees the right tools to do the job, and they will deliver what you ask.

The business case template provides a consistent way to look at projects. Because resource allocation is one of senior management's primary responsibilities, a consistent approach for analyzing projects will ensure that funding is properly allocated to those operating areas that will deliver the greatest value to the company. Management can then concentrate on understanding the content of the project and not on how the project is formatted. Without such an approach, individuals who review project proposals must continually reorient themselves each time a new format is presented. A consistent methodology for preparing a business case definitely lets management focus its attention on more substantive matters.

Perhaps one of the biggest benefits of following this book's guidance is the output itself. The comprehensive package that is assembled will become a continuing source of value for managing the project during its implementation, and it could become especially valuable should the scope of the project ever change. A thoroughly documented set of assumptions, sensitivity analysis and communications plan can quickly ground people on where the project is coming from and where it needs to go should conditions change.

Finally, measuring the effectiveness of the overall project development process, including the structuring of business cases, is an area of particular interest to many companies' internal auditing departments. The recommendations that are outlined will greatly improve the post-project auditing process and should help make your experience with internal auditing a pleasant one—should they ever desire to audit your project.

## WHO IS RESPONSIBLE?

Who in your organization is best qualified to prepare the business case? As you might suspect, there is no one right answer to this question because each project is different. The project manager or sponsor should designate the individual or individuals who will have lead responsibility for putting the package together. The leader can then delegate preparation of specific sections of the business case to other members of the project team, if desired. Use the Business Case Planning Guide on page 55 to help in the assigning and managing of individual responsibilities for completing the various sections of the business case.

It is quite common to have the project manager assume the lead role for preparing the business case. In these instances, the project manager typically delegates the financial analysis work to a financial analyst who is specifically assigned to support the project team. Because of the vast amount of financial-related information in the case, it is also not uncommon to see someone from the finance department assume responsibility for assembling the entire package. You can decide who is best positioned to coordinate this key function after reviewing the qualifications of the members of the project team. The following sections in this chapter will help orient the individuals who are selected to help build the business case.

# BUSINESS CASE PLANNING GUIDE

Overall Responsibility for Business Case: _____

*(list name)*

| Business Case Section | Primary Responsibility for Section *(list name)* | Other Required Support Staff *(list name)* | Reviewer of Finished Section *(list name)* | Timing – Due Date |
|---|---|---|---|---|
| **1. Executive Summary**<br>-Project Information<br>-Categorization<br>-Recommendation<br>-Project Description<br>-Financial Summary<br>-Abbreviated Timetable<br>-Approval Section | | | | |
| **2. Business Analysis**<br>-Statement of the Problem<br>-Discussion of Historical Context<br>-Discussion of Alternatives<br>-Fit with Goals & Strategy | | | | |
| **3. Financial Analysis**<br>-Income Statement & Cash Flows<br>-Evaluation of Cash Flows<br>-Cost Summary<br>-Benefit Summary<br>-Impact to Budget<br>-Financial Attestation | | | | |
| **4. What Can Go Wrong?**<br>-Top-Five Critical Drivers<br>-Sensitivity Analysis | | | | |
| **5. Impact Analysis**<br>-Impact on Other Departments<br>-Impact on Other Projects<br>-Impact on External Groups | | | | |
| **6. Project Management**<br>-Approval Hierarchy<br>-Project Team<br>-Project Manager<br>-Team Member Qualifications<br>-Timetable | | | | |
| **7. Appendix**<br>-Cost Checklists<br>-Benefit Checklists<br>-What Can Go Wrong Checklists<br>-Financial Evaluation Backup<br>-Glossary of Terms<br>-Alternative Comparison Matrix | | | | |

## EXECUTIVE SUMMARY

As you might have guessed by the title, the Executive Summary provides an overview of the financial and business reasons for your

Reviewed in Chapter 4

recommendation. This section is designed to impart just the right level of information to management, who may not have time to read the entire business case. Because of this, the Executive Summary is clearly the most important section in your business case. If you cannot do a good job summarizing the more salient points of your proposal, management will probably lose interest and fail to prioritize your project properly.

## BUSINESS ANALYSIS

The Business Analysis section explores the reasons why you have to do the project. It will help you document the problem that you are

Reviewed in Chapter 5

trying to solve or the business need you are trying to fulfill. This may not seem like a major issue in your mind, but I have repeatedly seen examples of projects that are best described as solutions in search of a problem. In other words, somebody has developed a great idea absent any clearly defined user need. Although they won't admit it, a lot of companies have a "spend it or lose it" culture when it comes to spending capital. Documenting and validating the business reasons behind a project can definitely help a company to better manage its costs. Only spend the money if there is a valid business need to do so.

## FINANCIAL ANALYSIS

While the Executive Summary is clearly the most important part in the business case, the Financial Analysis section comes in a close

Reviewed in Chapter 6

second when it comes to popularity. For the most part, the project will not get approved if it cannot meet the company's expectations for acceptable financial performance. The Financial Analysis chapter is extremely thorough and takes you through every step of the analytical process. Guidance is offered on how to develop cost and benefit assumptions and how to prepare the overall financial model. We will also review how to evaluate the data and interpret whether the results are meaningful. Helpful checklists

# Top Ten Reasons Not To Do A Project

10. We want to buy the product because the vendor always takes us out golfing.

9. Cool marketing brochures and good looking sales team.

8. The vendor's annual user conference is in Orlando.

7. Although the software doesn't do everything we want, the sales person said not to worry. The next release will take care of it.

6. If I don't use my entire capital budget I won't get as much money next year.

5. My kids really like Orlando.

4. Our project team has some extra time on its hands so we came up with a project to keep them busy.

3. Every other company is doing a project like this, and we don't want to be left out.

2. We already have a neat idea for a project team jacket and coffee mug; all we need is a project.

1. And did I mention the vendor's annual user conference is in Orlando?

are used extensively in this chapter to assist in the analysis. Additional information that further explains the financial concepts presented in the chapter is also included in several appendices of this book.

## WHAT CAN GO WRONG? (SENSITIVITY ANALYSIS)

A sensitivity analysis of the financial model is strongly recommended once you have completed the financial analysis. What kind of things can affect the project's outcome? What are the project's mission-critical drivers, and how sensitive are they to changing conditions? A thorough sensitivity analysis can help communicate the project's risk profile by documenting the potential variability of its key operating drivers. A checklist is provided in this chapter, as well, to assist you in asking the right questions.

*Reviewed in Chapter 7*

## IMPACT ANALYSIS

One of the primary reasons for project failures is poor communication. Projects often impact many departments throughout the company, and rarely are they ever self-contained within the sponsoring organization. This chapter addresses the communication and teamwork challenges facing every project. It is essential that the project's leadership increase their awareness as to how their project can impact people inside and outside the company. If they do not, then the project runs the risk of not being properly prioritized in the work queue when it comes time for acquiring resources.

*Reviewed in Chapter 8*

## PROJECT MANAGEMENT

This section of the business case involves a discussion on how the project will be managed once the go-ahead is given. This is the part of the case where the roles and responsibilities of the key players are defined and a preliminary timetable is presented. Although this section is meant to be brief, it will give management a sense of how organized the project team is in order to accomplish its mission. As a personal incentive for project managers, senior management will always display more confidence and support of project managers who can demonstrate that their projects are well organized.

*Reviewed in Chapter 9*

## THE BUSINESS CASE PYRAMID

## BUSINESS CASE APPENDIX

Any backup information that is needed to support the previous six sections of the business case should be included in the Appendix.

*Reviewed in Chapter 9*

This can include information such as the various checklists that are used, supplemental data supporting the financial evaluation or other information that helps to present a more complete picture of the project. Once you have completed this section, you are now in a position to fit all of the pieces of the business case puzzle together.

## CAUTION – KNOW THE RULES!

Before beginning any work on your business case, a word of caution is in order about rules. Many business activities are typically governed by some kind of procedure or corporate policy (although you may feel your company's capital process is one exception). Policies

and procedures can cover such things as the business case approval process, guidelines for project tracking and procedures for amending business cases. You must always be mindful, before you proceed with your work, of any policies your company may have on capital spending. If you are not aware of the rules, contact your accounting and finance department or the group responsible for maintaining corporate policies. **Do not start off on the wrong foot by violating company policy.** If your company does have policies or procedures already in place, talk with the governing organization about modifying the procedures to incorporate the guidance offered in this book. The process as outlined in this book is designed to work in any organization.

The situation definitely becomes more complex should you discover that your company has no policies or procedures governing capital spending. Although it may involve additional effort on your part, there is a golden opportunity here for you to recommend a formal process that could add tremendous value to the company. Work with your finance department to define the requirements and set the standards for analyzing business cases.

Having forewarned you about the necessity to investigate your company's policies, we can now turn our attention to actually building the business case. The first requirement on the path of preparing the business case is to examine the elements that are contained in the Executive Summary. As was said earlier, your project most likely will not get approved if it is not convincingly presented in the Executive Summary.

## PROJECT INFORMATION
Project Name:
Project Sponsor:
Project Manager:

## CATEGORIZATION

❑ New Business        ❑ General/Administrative
❑ Ongoing Support     ❑ Government Required
❑ Other: _____

## RECOMMENDATION
*Briefly state what it is you want to do. What do you want senior management to approve?*

## PROJECT DESCRIPTION
*Briefly describe the project including its objective and the nature of the costs and benefits.*

[Be mindful that the section numbers in the upper right corners of the business case templates do not correspond to the number of the chapters they are reviewed in. For instance, Business Case section 1 is reviewed in Chapter 4; section 2 is in Chapter 5, and so on.]

# THE EXECUTIVE SUMMARY

As the name suggests, the Executive Summary is meant to summarize the project's key information into two or three pages for review by those senior managers who will be approving the project. The material in this summary will provide an excellent introduction to the in-depth analysis that is to follow in the business case. As was said earlier, the Executive Summary is the most important part of the business case. If it isn't done well, it can lead to either an immediate rejection of the project or a painful review of many project details.

Although the Executive Summary is the first part of the business case, it should be the last part you complete. Having said that, don't get the idea to skip over this section. It is important for you to review this material first because it will give you a "flavor" for the key information that you will need to summarize as you work through the chapters that follow. As you review the various sections in this chapter, it will become obvious why this section must be done last.

The Executive Summary includes seven parts:

1. Project Information
2. Categorization
3. Recommendation
4. Project Description
5. Financial Summary
6. Abbreviated Timetable
7. Approval Section

## PROJECT INFORMATION

Put the name of the project here along with the names of the project's sponsor and manager. If the project was previously known by another name, list that here as well.

See template on page 62

## CATEGORIZATION

Many companies feel the need to classify their projects into pre-defined categories that are usually aligned with the organization's strategic goals.

See template on page 62

Categorizing projects in such a manner can greatly aid in prioritizing work. It can also position the company to focus its resources into more strategically important areas should the company ever face financial difficulties.

The categories in Example 1 demonstrate how a company's strategic business objectives are used as a means for labeling projects. Of course, your company may have different strategic classifications that can be substituted for those shown in the example. Many businesses prefer to use the classifications as shown in Example 2, although a word of caution is in order. I do not recommend following this

---

**Example 1**

**Project Classifications**

- ❑  New business
- ❑  Ongoing support
- ❑  General and Administrative
- ❑  Government Required

---
**Example 2**
**Project Classifications**

❑ Discretionary
❑ Non-Discretionary

---

example and advise against using any kind of categorization that attempts to judge. Asking people to categorize their project as discretionary versus non-discretionary is similar to asking them whether their project is really important or is it just "make work." It will not take managers long to figure out which category is the *correct* answer.

4

## RECOMMENDATION

The Recommendation section should briefly state what you want from senior management. You will find that this section is highly correlated to those See template on page 62 items or activities that will be purchased for your project. Limit your recommendation to a few concise sentences. Tell management exactly what you plan to do with the money that they will give you.

---
EXAMPLE RECOMMENDATION

Management approval is requested for the installation of a new computer network that will support the Company's fifty field offices. This proposal also requests funding for the extensive training the field offices will need in order to implement the new system.

---

## PROJECT DESCRIPTION

Relative to the Project Recommendation, the Project Description offers the reader more information as to the how and why of what it is the project is trying to accomplish. This section should describe, in a very succinct manner, the objectives of the project and the nature of its costs and benefits. A helpful format to follow is to answer these questions:

See template on page 62

- ✧ What is the project trying to accomplish?

- ✧ Why is it important that this project be done?

- ✧ How will the project team accomplish its mission?

---

EXAMPLE DESCRIPTION

WOMBAT Sales System

The project will purchase and install the new sales system. This new system automates order taking and will give the company a distinct advantage vis-à-vis the competition, which is projected to implement a similar system within the next two years. WOMBAT automates processes that are currently done manually, and it also provides internet connectivity for our customers. The system will run on the Company's existing network. It is projected to increase sales by 10% and reduce back-office support by 25%. A comprehensive training program is planned that will support an accelerated project rollout. The projected cost of the project is $1.2 million over an eighteen month period.

Although these are some very big questions, that could invite a big response, you should strive to keep this section to no more than half of a page. Obviously, it will take some effort to capture the essence of each question's answer in two or three sentences. Remember that senior management can always turn to the detail in the appropriate section of the business case if they desire additional information.

## FINANCIAL SUMMARY

This part will be easy to complete once you have finished the Financial Analysis section of the case. Simply insert into the spreadsheet the key financial indicators your company wishes to follow. Typically, this includes the net income and cash flow generated by the project. *See template on page 68* The timeline for the spreadsheet is generally equal to the life span of the project. (There will be more about this in the Financial Analysis chapter of the book.)

You should also include in this section the total capital outlay that is being requested and the financial measures used to evaluate the project. These metrics could include NPV (net present value), IRR (internal rate of return), payback or many others. These terms will become clearer once you have read the Financial Analysis chapter. The final part of this section asks whether any of the project's proposed spending is included in the company's budget. There are only three choices here ("yes," "no" or "partially"), which will be of great interest to management.

Because every company uses slightly different methods for analyzing projects, you can easily tailor this section to the unique methods that your company has for evaluating projects. Always remember to keep the information at a ***very high level***. The Financial Analysis chapter in the business case will provide greater detail if management needs it.

## EXECUTIVE SUMMARY    *Business Case Part1.x*

### FINANCIAL SUMMARY

|  | Present Year | Year 1 | Year 2 | Year 3... (through the life of the project) |
|---|---|---|---|---|
| Net Income | $ | | | |
| Cash Flow | $ | | | |

Capital Investment:
NPV @ ___% Discount Rate:
IRR:
Payback:
Capital Investment Included in Budget? ❏ Yes ❏ No ❏ Partially

*You will tailor this section to the financial methods that you will be using for evaluating your project. The financial methods are reviewed in Chapter 6. Always keep the information at a very high level.*

### ABBREVIATED TIMETABLE

Start Date:
Major Milestone Dates:
Finish Date:

*Include the starting and ending dates of the project at a minimum. You may also include the dates of any significant milestones if known.*

## ABBREVIATED TIMETABLE

The abbreviated timetable is meant to give management a sense of how long it will take to complete the
project. Include the starting and ending dates at a
minimum and also the dates of any significant milestones if the team has them identified. If financial
projections were made for the project, then these dates will be readily
available. The financial projections could not have been made
without them.

See
template
on page
68

4

## APPROVAL SECTION

The final part of the Executive Summary is where
management gets to "sign on the dotted line." This
section is segmented into two parts:

See
template
on page
70

❖ Project authorization

❖ Impacted area approval

The project authorization area should include the signature
blocks for the normal approval hierarchy in your company. (Chapter
11 provides valuable insight on how you can obtain a speedy
approval from senior management.) The impacted area approval is
reserved for the signatures of managers from key organizations that
are affected in some way by the project. (Chapter 8 provides guidance on how you should address this section.)

## FINISHING TOUCHES TO THE BUSINESS CASE PACKAGE

Before moving onto the rest of the business case, there are a few
"cosmetic niceties" that you should prepare:

❖ The Business Case Cover page

❖ Table of Contents page

These two additions will give the business case a most professional look. Consider this part of your product packaging. And as we
all know, good-looking products sell better than bad-looking ones.

## EXECUTIVE SUMMARY                                    *1.x*

### APPROVAL SECTION

Project Authorization

_____    _____
Name & Title                        Date

_____    _____
Name & Title                        Date

_____    _____
Name & Title                        Date

_____    _____
Name & Title                        Date

### IMPACTED AREA APPROVAL

_____    _____
Name & Title & Organization         Date

_____    _____
Name & Title & Organization         Date

_____    _____
Name & Title & Organization         Date

*Include signature blocks for the normal approval hierarchy in your
company. Also provide an approval section for the managers of any
key areas impacted by the project.*

## THE BUSINESS CASE PYRAMID

It is important to reiterate that the Executive Summary should only be completed once the other parts of the business case are finished. Having read this chapter, you now have a good sense of the key information that must be extracted from your case in order to make an effective Executive Summary. The business case is like a pyramid, as was shown in the "pieces of the puzzle" diagram in Chapter 3. The Business Analysis, Financial Analysis and other sections of the case provide support for the Executive Summary that is at the top. And in order to begin building the business case pyramid, one has to start by laying a key foundation block, which is examining the reasoning for doing the project. The next chapter helps you to prepare a cohesive story on why the project is being done in the first place.

## (Your Project Name Here)
# BUSINESS CASE

*Prepared by:*
*Organization:*

*Date:*

# TABLE OF CONTENTS

*Substitute the appropriate page number for the* **X** *that is shown above. For example, if the Executive Summary has four pages, they should be marked:* **1.1, 1.2 … 1.4**

## STATEMENT OF THE PROBLEM/ISSUE/OPPORTUNITY
*Provide a concise statement of the problem, issue or opportunity the project is trying to resolve or act upon.*

## DISCUSSION OF HISTORICAL CONTEXT
*Include any prior history of the project here, especially if the project experienced difficulties in the past.*

## DISCUSSION OF ALTERNATIVES CONSIDERED

Lower-Cost Alternative: *Are there ways to address the problem if you were only given half the money?*

Higher-Cost Alternative: *What ways could you address the problem if money is no object?*

Do-Nothing Alternative: *What is the impact of delaying the project one year?*

## FIT WITH COMPANY GOALS & STRATEGY
*How does the project fit with goals and strategy of the company?*

# Business Analysis –
# Show Me the Reasoning

The one thing that seems to be missing in most business cases is the reasoning behind the recommendation for the proposed project. Usually there is a logical thought process behind the choice, but most of the time it is never documented. The approver or reader of the business case is often left to wonder as to the origins of the project.

The Business Analysis section addresses the idea or conceptualization stage of the project and lays the groundwork for the financial analysis that is to follow. This section conveys to the reader of the business case why the project has come into existence. It discusses the problem, issue or opportunity the project hopes to address for the company. And it also reviews the history surrounding the project. Is this a new idea or has the company tried something similar in the past?

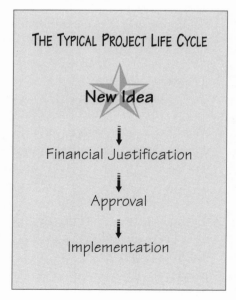

THE TYPICAL PROJECT LIFE CYCLE

**New Idea**

↓

Financial Justification

↓

Approval

↓

Implementation

This section also examines the other alternatives that are available and how you evaluated them. The Business Analysis section of the business case provides an excellent opportunity to highlight the extensive process you worked through to arrive at your recommendation.

Whenever people are asked to provide background information on a project idea they always seem to wonder how much information is enough. Your objective should be to prepare a concise summary that conveys a sufficient understanding of the origins of the project. Because this section can get quite long if you are not careful, you should structure your business analysis in the following manner:

✧ Problem, issue or opportunity identification

✧ Discussion of the historical context

✧ Alternatives considered

✧ Fit with company goals and strategy

## STATE THE PROBLEM, ISSUE OR OPPORTUNITY

This section in your business case discusses the problem or issue the project hopes to solve or the business opportunity the project seeks to exploit. For example, assume that you discovered a weakness in a competitor's product lineup that you feel your company can take advantage of by making just a few modifications to its existing products. The project may involve modifying the product as well as planning for the additional sales and marketing support needed to put the new idea in the marketplace. The business case should present the bigger picture as to why the project is being done. This example would be considered incomplete if you left out the reason and only stated that your project involved making some product modifications that needed to be supported by the company's sales and marketing teams. The project reviewers need to know **why** the project is being considered in the first place.

The example just reviewed involved discovering an opportunity and developing a project to take advantage of it. Another example could involve addressing a pressing problem for the company. Complying with government regulations is an example of an area that creates many issues for companies. For projects dealing with government compliance matters it is especially important that your business case discuss the bigger picture. These types of projects most likely have little or no financial merit (although cost avoidance may be substantial), and it is therefore critical to highlight the mandatory external conditions driving the decision. Do not assume that the reader of the business case understands the problem you are trying to solve. Write it down!

## DISCUSSION OF THE HISTORICAL CONTEXT

This section seeks to answer a simple question. Does the project address an issue that is new to the company, or is it another attempt to resolve old business? Has the company tried to implement slightly different versions of your project idea in the past? An individual reviewing the project would analyze the proposal differently depending on whether it is a brand-new idea or if it is just today's attempt to solve yesterday's problem. A different set of questions must be asked of projects whose paths are littered with previous failed attempts. It is wise to remember the old saying, "Those who don't remember the past are doomed to repeat it." This section should alert the approver to any historical events that may have an impact on the present decision making process.

# REPEATING THE PAST...

During the time when laptop computers were becoming popular, a financial services company had a great idea for a project that would automate their mortgage company's loan origination process. Loan agents would be able to complete most of the paperwork right on their laptop computers as they interviewed their customers. It was a great idea, but the project failed miserably (for many reasons) with the company spending tens of millions of dollars.

After some time had passed and numerous management changes, the project surfaced again—this time with a brand new name and no mention of its checkered past. The project's "second life" did not fare any better. It was also cancelled after spending another sizable sum of money.

If management had been aware of the second project's dismal past, they probably never would have approved it unless a thorough "autopsy" of the first project was conducted. The second project should have discussed the first failure and perhaps included a special section that discussed "what went wrong?" and "lessons learned."

## Discussion of Alternatives Considered

There is always more than one way to tackle a problem or to take advantage of a new opportunity. Unfortunately most project managers or sponsors rarely include any discussion of alternative approaches in their business cases. Most claim they are too busy to prepare scenarios that will not be implemented. Instead they would rather focus their energy on the recommended project. This seems like a valid argument, so why is it important to review other alternatives?

One of the responsibilities of the project manager during the project's conceptual stage is to be open to different ways to solve problems. Diligent and broad-minded managers are always open to new ideas. Creating other options for solving your problem may even lead to unexpected breakthroughs in other parts of the company. I have seen one case where an alternative sparked tremendous interest in an operating area that was previously unconnected with the original project. The discussion of a different course of action caused this operating group to lobby for and eventually change the scope of the project under review.

Another typical comeback from project managers who do not want to document their options is, "Here's my recommendation. I've considered all the options, but I am too busy to explain them to you. You don't need to worry though. I know I have selected the best solution for the company. Trust me." Most reviewers do not want to put themselves into the position of saying, "I don't trust you," even though they may think that. Instead, you should institute a policy that requires every project proposal to include a discussion of the alternatives. By asking for documented alternatives, you would not have to question anyone's trustworthiness—it would just be company policy.

There are three all-purpose options that are extremely effective for providing structure around the definition of the alternatives. In addition to the preferred solution, you should review a *lower-cost* alternative, a *higher-cost* alternative and a *do-nothing* alternative. An example will help illuminate each alternative.

## EXAMINING THE ALTERNATIVES: AN EXAMPLE

Suppose you are a member of the corporate finance department in your company, and the problem you are trying to solve is the lack of a company-wide standard for preparing capital project business cases. The Chief Financial Officer believes that the non-standard approach presently employed by the company leads to poor decision making during the capital budgeting process. She also feels the poor decision making ultimately hurts the company strategically and financially. If the preferred solution were to outline a process as recommended in this book, one could envision the three alternatives to be:

## LOWER-COST ALTERNATIVE

Instead of consulting with outside resources for guidance on this matter, the corporate finance department could develop simple spreadsheet templates for preparing the project's financial justification. This material would then be disseminated to all operating areas with minimal instruction in order to keep the cost down. For example, there would not be any centralized guidance on how to develop the business cases. Business case evaluation would focus only on the financial justification.

The purpose of the low-cost solution is to have you think of ways to address the problem if you were only given *half* of the money requested. Could you still develop a solution that would provide value if your resources were severely constrained?

## HIGHER-COST ALTERNATIVE

A higher-cost solution to the CFO's problem is to develop a sophisticated computer application using programmers from the company's information technology department. The programmers estimate the development will take one year if the requirements are clearly documented and do not change. The programming, hardware and software costs could get excessive, and the user acceptance of the output is uncertain. A standard software solution, however, could greatly improve the company's overall capital budgeting process.

The higher-cost solution is meant to provide a "money is no object" option. What would you propose if you had unlimited resources? The truly creative, leading-edge solutions usually appear under these kinds of scenarios. Do not let the 'resources-are-limited' straight jacket keep you from ideas that could propel your company into new frontiers.

## Do-Nothing Alternative

This alternative is often called the base case. In our example, the company would have no corporate-wide standard for preparing busi-ness cases if things stayed the same. Each operating area would continue with its own specialized way of analyzing and preparing business cases. A hybrid alternative that is strongly recommended is to challenge whether the project can be deferred one year. What is the risk to the company of slipping the timing of the project? Having the option to delay spending is extremely valuable because funds earmarked for the project can be directed to other time-sensitive initiatives.

It is not intended that you provide a full business case for each alternative in this analysis, only a high-level discussion of each option and its strategic impact. Although not shown in the example, you should also include a rough approximation of the financial requirements for each option. Documenting the alternatives provides the project team protection from going down the wrong path, and it also ensures that the team's vision is aligned with senior management's thinking. Completing this section in your business case is considered valuable insurance should your project ever run into trouble and the 'second guessers' claim you implemented the wrong solution. You can quickly remove any doubt as to why you selected your project by referring them to the Business Analysis section in your business case.

## FIT WITH COMPANY GOALS AND STRATEGY

Does your company have a strategic plan? When asked, most senior executives would almost always answer: "Of course we do!" Given this kind of response one would think it would be rather easy to show how a project fits into the corporate strategy. Documenting how the project specifically relates to the strategic plan is very difficult in practice, however. People are often unwilling to admit to this difficulty because it would reveal how out of touch they are with their own company's plan. The purpose of this section in your business case is to explain how your project supports the company's operating goals and strategy. My experience has shown that, despite its simple objective, many project managers have tremendous difficulty completing this section.

A good example of how this concept is applied in practice is in the automobile industry. One goal that automotive manufacturers must manage is the overall fuel efficiency of the vehicles they produce. As each new vehicle is designed, the company can calculate how that vehicle's fuel efficiency affects the government-mandated, corporate average fuel efficiency goal. A new product recommendation is not considered complete unless the vehicle's impact on the corporate goal is addressed in the proposal.

Prepare yourself for a barrage of questions if your proposal adversely affects the company's strategic goals. If you have no idea what your company's strategic plan is or your management considers it top-secret and not for distribution, consider the following advice:

## THE ULTIMATE GOAL OF ANY PROJECT IS TO INCREASE SHAREHOLDER VALUE.

Explain, in non-financial and high-level financial terms, how your project increases the value of the company.

Completing the Business Analysis section of the business case is extremely important because it explains the reasoning behind the project. Since management seldom has time to keep abreast of all the company's projects, this section will be most welcomed by them when it comes time to grant approval. Having reviewed the rationale for proposing the project, the attention now turns to the financial analysis. How much financial value does the project deliver to the company?

❖

# FINANCIAL ANALYSIS

The Financial Analysis section of the business case includes the following parts:

1. Income Statement and Cash Flows

2. Evaluation of Cash Flows

3. Cost Summary

4. Benefit Summary

5. Financial Attestation

6. Impact to Budget

*These sections are reviewed in detail in Chapter 6, and the business case templates can be found on pages 89, 99, 116, 138, and 140.*

# 6

# FINANCIAL ANALYSIS – SHOW ME THE MONEY

> *"Unfortunately, there is a real danger of becoming immersed in excessive complexity and losing sight of some basic computations that can be very helpful in evaluating capital projects."*
> — BIERMAN AND SMIDT, THE CAPITAL BUDGETING DECISION

The Financial Analysis section is usually the most critical section of the business case. For many companies it is typically the *only* section of their business case. While it is important to understand the project's impact on the business strategy, it still winds down to "show me the money" at the end of the day. What value does the project create for the company?

What does it mean when someone says you need to show how the project adds value to the company? For a moment, pretend you are the sole owner of a small company that is completely self-sufficient. You do not have to rely on any external financing in order to run the business. Because you control the "purse strings," you might dispense with the need to do intricate project analysis and justification. If you felt a project added value (however you defined it), you would simply do the project. Now let us suppose that your company doesn't make enough money to pay for the capital projects it wishes to do. Any capital programs would now have to be funded by borrowing from external sources such as banks. And banks, of course, will not just take your word that your projects will add value. You will have to prove the merits of each case during the bank's loan process. This proof usually takes the form of a formal financial presentation that goes to a loan committee for approval.

Because bankers are typically risk averse by nature, the loan request must be well documented, justified and of the highest quality. *[On a personal note, anyone who has ever applied for a home loan can relate to this demanding experience.]* The loan request that you prepare for your business is called the business case. A thorough Financial Analysis section in your business case will help convince your "bankers" of your project's merit thereby making them more willing to loan you the money. I am not suggesting here that you need to hire a banker to review your project proposal. "Banker" is just a term to denote the source of the money. The need to prepare a business case is created when the source of the money to fund your project comes from someone else and not out of your own wallet. Who in your company would you call the "banker"?

You should always prepare your business cases with a "banker's" mindset—very demanding for documentation and wanting to minimize risk. However, bankers know that risk can never be completely eliminated. The key is how well can you minimize your ***exposure*** to risk. Your business case, particularly the Financial Analysis section, should help answer the following questions from the banker's perspective:

✧ Why should I loan you the money?

✧ How can I trust your proposal?

✧ What's in it for me?

The purpose of this chapter is to prepare a financial presentation that will convince your "banker" to loan you the money for your project. Again, the banker could be an external or an internal lender. The banker may also happen to be you. How would you want your employees evaluating project decisions that ultimately spend your money?

Your financial presentation must meet several basic requirements. The analysis must be accurate, thorough and demonstrate good financial theory. You must also structure the information in a way that easily communicates the financial merits of the project. The diagram on page 82 shows what information is required in the Finan-cial Analysis section and the order in which it should be presented in the business case. The templates for this section are on pages 89, 99, 116, 138, and 140.

This chapter will cover the material in a slightly different order, however:

1. Cost Summary
2. Benefits Summary
3. Income Statement and Cash Flows
4. Evaluation of Cash Flows
5. Financial Attestation
6. Impact to Budget

It is important to proceed in this manner because the cost and benefits summaries are the building blocks for everything else. The cost and benefit data are used in the preparation of the income and cash flow statement, which subsequently produces the Financial Summary in the Executive Summary.

The sections in the Financial Analysis chapter represent a fun-damental set of processes that are easily adaptable to any company's

## The Finance Pyramid

project evaluation process, regardless of its uniqueness. To the extent your company has a special evaluation tool or procedure, simply plug it into the financial analysis framework. Inserting any unique company requirements only enhances its effectiveness because the overall process intuitively makes sense and is reasonable. Again, you would demand no less rigor if it was *your* money being spent.

Although the Executive Summary is the primary section in the business case that management wants to see, the Financial Analysis section will turn out to be one of the most scrutinized sections. For the most part, how well the Financial Analysis is prepared will determine the "go" or "no-go" decision for funding the project.

If you do not have a finance background, it will not be possible for you to complete this chapter on your own. You will have to ask for assistance from your finance department or the financial analyst supporting your group. But don't interpret this as a convenient excuse to transfer all responsibility to Finance. The individual designated to manage the overall preparation of the business case should continue to oversee this section closely—even when big parts of it are "outsourced" to someone in a finance group.

As you go through this chapter, you will find many invitations to read about financial analysis concepts in the Appendix. I strongly encourage you to read them so you can become better versed on this most critical function. (Financial analysts should also give these sections a close look. They will find them most informative should they desire to "brush up" on their project analysis skills or discuss these concepts with their clients.)

## Handling the Rough Times

When it comes to building a house most people generally acknowledge that cutting corners on laying a good foundation only comes back to haunt you. It may seem more efficient at the time, but you will pay dearly for those shortcuts when problems start to surface in later years. Preparing a financial analysis is similar in many respects although the problems generally surface a lot sooner.

Just as construction problems are inevitable when building a house, you should anticipate that your project **will** incur some difficulties during implementation. And as issues arise, communicating changes in the financial projections becomes a critical and mandatory requirement. How well those changes are communicated often depends on how well the starting point of the financial analysis was prepared. If you did a poor job on the initial analysis, you are going to have a most difficult time communicating your project's financial needs to senior management.

As one might expect, senior management has little tolerance for project modifications. They are often skeptical of project changes because project costs always seem to go up thereby driving returns down. Rarely does management ever receive "good news" on project performance. A stronger financial analysis will not eliminate all the problems a project may encounter, but it will make it easier to communicate the incremental request for funding that is often sought. When it comes to dealing with project modifications, management always seems to react better when presented with the following information:

Step 1: Here's what the project originally involved and what it cost

Step 2: Here's what changed and why

Step 3: Here's what we now need to do and what it will cost

It will be all but impossible to lay out your new request if you did not prepare a very solid financial analysis in Step 1. By cutting corners on the process, all you are doing is shifting your work to the back end of the project when "damage control" will become necessary to handle the inevitable accusations of project mismanagement. You can avoid the need for "damage control" by keeping management well informed of Steps 1-3 outlined above.

You greatly increase the risk of undermining the intended results of your project (as well as severely annoying management) by not building a solid financial foundation. And as many can personally attest, problem programs always cost the company more in the long run, both financially and strategically.

6

## COST SUMMARY

The best place to begin your financial analysis is to examine your project's costs. It is always a lot easier for people to determine how they will spend money (project costs) versus how they will save or generate money (project benefits). Project costs represent the out-flows of cash that typically occur early in the project's life cycle. They generally fall into a couple of classifications:

♦ Capital Investment costs
♦ Implementation costs
♦ Depreciation
♦ Other costs

Capital Investment costs include the assets that are purchased, and Implementation costs generally include the labor-related ex-penses associated with working on the project. Depreciation is the cost associated with the project's assets (more about this later), and the Other costs category is meant to capture anything that doesn't neatly fit into the prior three categories.

Your analysis should include only those costs that are incremen-tal to your business operations. For example, do not include the labor costs of internal personnel if you could be using them for something else. You would include the labor in your analysis if the costs for those individuals would go away if the project did not exist (i.e. you would terminate the labor). The best way to think about what to include is to, again, imagine yourself as the banker. Visualize what additional money you would have to pull out of your wallet in order to support the project. The items that cause you to spend the additional money are the things that you should include in the cost section. It does not matter at this point how the accounting department will capitalize or expense each item. [An asset's cost is considered capitalized when its value is spread over the asset's useful life. For example, an asset (with a five-year life span) costing $100,000 is said to be capitalized when its costs are reflected in the financial statements over a period of five years (i.e. $20,000 per year). If the costs were all expensed, the com-pany would reflect a $100,000 expense in the year the asset was pur-chased.] Our only interest is in the items affecting cash flow (i.e. the money coming out of the company "wallet").

The template for the cost section is shown on page 89. Input the

# FINANCIAL ANALYSIS                                    3.x

## COST SUMMARY

|  | Initial Investment | Year 1 | Year 2... (through the life of the project) |
|---|---|---|---|
| Cost Item A | | | |
| Cost Item B | | | |
| Cost Item C | | | |
| Total Capital Investment Costs | | | |
| | | | |
| Cost Item D | | | |
| Cost Item E | | | |
| Cost Item F | | | |
| Cost Item G | | | |
| Cost Item H | | | |
| Total Implementation Costs | | | |
| | | | |
| Depreciation | | | |
| | | | |
| Other | | | |
| | | | |
| Total Costs | | | |

*Provide a summary of your project cost assumptions. It will help to categorize your costs where possible as is shown in this example.*

names of the cost items (and their respective financial data) for each category. Of course, you should use more appropriate categories if the ones on the template do not apply for your company. The checklists that follow will assist you in evaluating each cost item.

## COST CHECKLISTS

After itemizing all of your project costs in the Cost Summary (but before you actually calculate the financial amounts), you should "run" each of your anticipated costs through the Cost Checklists. The Cost Checklists are questionnaires that will help you to analyze your cost assumptions and build credibility into your financial projections. They are divided into four parts:

✧ Description and derivation
✧ Cost competitiveness
✧ Accounting treatment
✧ Assumption sensitivity section

The checklists will assist you in conducting a thorough examination of the accuracy of your assumptions. They will also serve as a vehicle for documenting your work as well as raising potential communication and people issues that could surface and impact the assumptions.

**Complete a Cost Checklist for each item listed on the project cost summary.** This will help you to thoroughly document all of the cost assumptions. This may seem like a lot of work, especially if your project is big, but quality time spent on developing your project's assumptions will return handsomely for those assuming project management roles.

Although these checklists do not provide an exhaustive listing of questions for every type of business situation, they are fairly representative of issues faced by many businesses. The checklists are very adaptable and can be modified to better suit your particular needs. There is also no need to answer every question. Simply check the appropriate response, or only answer those questions that add value to your cost analysis. The cost checklists all share a common format and are short in length and very user friendly. Again, use the checklists for every cost assumed in the business case. If you have five cost elements, then you will use these checklists *five* times. Include the

## Cost Item Process Flow

Complete the four cost checklists
for each item in the Cost Summary

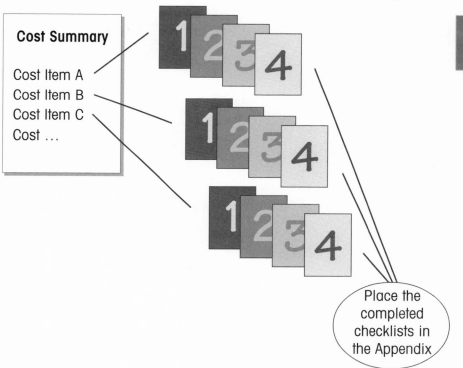

6

**Cost Summary**

Cost Item A
Cost Item B
Cost Item C
Cost ...

Place the
completed
checklists in
the Appendix

answers to the checklist questions in the appendix of your business case in case management cares to examine the derivation of the assumptions.

The purpose of the first Cost Checklist is to thoroughly document the nature of the cost item under review. This includes explaining how the amount and timing were determined as well as who is in control of the cost. Several items on this checklist (the ones with only a 'yes' option) are mandatory requirements that every project must address.

# Cost Checklist 1: Description & Derivation

Cost Item: _____ *(Run each cost through this checklist)*

| Number | Applies to Project | Review Topic | Guidance/Action |
|---|---|---|---|
| 1 | ❑ Yes | Cost description | Describe the nature and amount of the cost in simple terms. (e.g. If you need a vehicle for your project, don't just write "car." Include the make, model, options and cost.) |
| 2 | ❑ Yes | Cost classification<br>❑ Capital Investment<br>❑ Implementation Cost<br>❑ Ongoing Support Costs<br>❑ Other | Is the cost one-time in nature or will it be recurring? |
| 3 | ❑ Yes | Timing of spending | Over what period of time will the money be spent? How was the timing determined? |
| 4 | ❑ Yes  ❑ No | Inflation | Have you factored inflation into your cost assumption? |
| 5 | ❑ Yes  ❑ No | Taxes | Are there any taxes associated with this assumption (sales, property, use taxes)? If yes, show the calculation. |
| 6 | ❑ Yes | Cost calculation | Show and explain the derivation of the cost estimate (do the math). |
| 7 | ❑ Yes | Cost ownership | Who in the organization is responsible for this assumption? Will this cost be under the direct control of the project manager or does it involve someone outside of the project's control? |
| 8 | ❑ Yes  ❑ No<br>❑ Not Applicable | Labor-related costs | For people-related costs (internal employees, temporaries or contractors), how did you estimate the time required for completing the task? Do you have to hire anyone? If yes, you will need to evaluate the risk of adding payment staff. |

The second Cost Checklist attempts to determine the reasonableness of the cost estimate. How does the company know whether the estimate is not exaggerated?

## Cost Checklist 2: Cost Competitiveness

Cost Item:_____    *(Run each cost through this checklist)*

| Number | Applies to Project | Review Topic | Guidance/Action |
|--------|--------------------|--------------|-----------------|
| 1 | ❑ Yes  ❑ No | Benchmaking | Does your company have any benchmarking data for this cost? How will they know the cost is reasonable? |
| 2 | ❑ Yes  ❑ No  ❑ Not Required | Competitive bid | Was the cost put out for competitive bid? If your company has a policy for competitive bidding then state whether you have complied. How many and which companies were involved? Where are you in the process? Did you quote the list price or have you already negotiated the price? |

Cost Checklist 3 is designed to make you think about how the accounting department handles the cost once the money is actually spent. A key question that must be addressed is "who pays?"

## Cost Checklist 3: Accounting Treatment

Cost Item:_____    *(Run each cost through this checklist)*

| Number | Applies to Project | Review Topic | Guidance/Action |
|--------|--------------------|--------------|-----------------|
| 1 | ❑ Expense  ❑ Capital  ❑ Don't Know | Expense vs. Capital | Will the cost be expensed or capitalized? |
| 2 | ❑ Yes  ❑ No  ❑ Not Required | Accounting consultation | Did you meet with the accounting department to discuss the accounting treatment or did you guess? If yes, with whom did you meet? |
| 3 | ❑ Yes | Posting of costs | What specific operating area in the company will incur the cost? Where will the cost be posted on the general ledger? Is that area aware that this cost will be assigned to their cost center? |

## Cost Checklist 4: Assumption Sensitivity

Cost Item: _____   *(Run each cost through this checklist)*

| Number | Applies to Project | Review Topic | Guidance/Action |
|---|---|---|---|
| 1 | ❑ Yes | Assumption sensitivity | What things can cause this assumption to change? List the cost drivers, and explain the range of possible outcomes. |
| 2 | ❑ Yes ❑ No | Outside vendor costs | If you are using an outside vendor, what are the risks associated with the vendor? Are you their first client? Is the vendor financially sound? |
| 3 | ❑ Yes ❑ No | Cost control | If this cost is under the control of an organization external to the project, will there be any resource allocation or work priority issues? |

The output that is developed from these checklists will be used in the income statement summary that management sees. These checklists give management the flexibility to quickly "drill down" into the detail should they have any questions on the financial summary. You will probably hate answering the checklists if you are not use to documenting your assumptions. If your blood pressure is going up just thinking about documenting your assumptions, stop and again revisit why you are doing this.

## These checklists will help you and your project succeed.

One of the ways you can increase the odds for achieving success is to minimize the risk inherent in the project. And you can better understand and communicate the project's overall risk profile only by thoroughly examining each cost element. The checklists are designed to facilitate that process.

In addition to the items included in the checklists, there are several other areas to keep in mind when developing your cost assumptions. These include incorporating probability into your estimates, inflation effects, sunk costs, opportunity costs, and the potential double counting of financing costs. Please refer to the section called **Other Cost Assumption Guidance** in Appendix 5 of this book. This section offers an in-depth (but easy to read) discussion of these most important items. Consider it mandatory reading for anyone who is charged with preparing the cost analysis.

**6**

## Setting the Project Timeline — Part I

As you begin your financial analysis one immediate issue you will face is determining the time frame to use for your projections. Should the company set a standard five or ten year time horizon when analyzing projects? The general rule of thumb is to use a period of time equal to the expected life of the project. If your project has an expected life of ten years, your analysis  should calculate cash flows for those ten years. But often times it is difficult to estimate the expected life span of a project. If you are dealing with a technology project, for example, the expected life may be as short as one or two years. Always keep in mind that the new, cutting edge project you are implementing today could easily become tomorrow's boat anchor because of technologic obsolescence. Be leery of projects with long expected lives.

Seek out one of your company's more experienced project managers for advice if you are not sure what time frame to use in your analysis. You can also talk to someone in your accounting department who is responsible for

managing fixed assets. They are the holders of the guidelines for setting depreciation rates on your company's
fixed assets. It is usually a good idea anyway to cross-
check the estimate of your project's life span with this
group to ensure consistency in your working assumptions.
The last thing you want to see is the accounting department using a depreciation schedule that differs from the
one in the project proposal seen by senior management.

Although developing the cost assumptions for a project seems
rather daunting, it is the developing of the benefits assumptions that
gives management the real big headaches. Costs are easier to think
about because they represent items or activities that require the
spending of money. And as we all know, the spending of money is
highly scrutinized in most companies. Benefits on the other hand are
promises, and promises by definition are highly uncertain. If the
project proposes to increase the company's revenues or lower its costs
for example, management wants to be reasonably assured that these
events will occur. Completing the Benefit Checklists will assist you
in providing that assurance.

## Setting the Project Timeline – Part II

Setting the length of time to evaluate the proposal is
normally not that complicated. What tends to confuse people is selecting a time frame when alternative
projects are also considered. In such cases it is important
to use timelines that are similar.
This is often difficult because
some of the alternatives may have
assets with different service lives.
There are no firm rules on setting
the time frame for this kind of

**6**

analysis, but generally speaking, you should strive to use the shortest period possible. The longer the time period, the more uncertainty there is in the assumptions. You should therefore try to minimize the number of assumptions (and accompanying uncertainty) for each alternative. The following example is provided to demonstrate the choices you have in selecting the time frame for the analysis. The length of time for each alternative reflects the asset's projected useful life if one were just examining the project by itself.

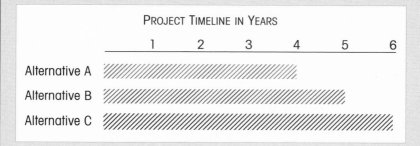

Given the choices, how many years should the analysis cover—4 years, 5 years, 6 years or something longer? If you were to select 4 years for your financial analysis it will become necessary to calculate the terminal value (or the remaining value that is left) of the assets in alternatives B and C. This is necessary because the life spans of those assets were artificially shortened by our analysis. Although their lives were shortened to 4 years, the assets in alternatives B and C continue to have value because you might be able to sell or lease them to someone else. This may be difficult in practice, but theoretically it is possible. Calculating the terminal value involves accounting for the assets' salvage value as well as the value associated with any remaining life (i.e. alternative B has 1 year of life remaining and alternative C has 2 years). You should consult with the fixed asset analyst in your accounting department to help determine an appropriate value for these assets.

If you were to select 5 years as the time frame for your financial analysis, alternative C would be treated the same way as mentioned above except the remaining life would be one year. What you should do with alternative A is not so clear since its life span is one year shorter than alternative B. You could decide to repurchase the assets at the end of year 4 and then calculate the terminal value as described above at year 5. Or you can examine other means of filling that one-year gap such as buying excess capacity from some other company. A preferred solution will usually surface as you proceed through the business and financial analysis of all the alternatives. Focus the analysis around the preferred alternative, and make the time frame of the other choices conform to the recommended project if at all possible. If there is no leading contender among the alternatives, try to minimize the time frame of the analysis.

## BENEFIT SUMMARY

Benefits are the promises managers and sponsors of projects make to senior management that gives them the right to spend the owner's money. Benefits are also the primary reason a project is undertaken. Despite these two significant facts, benefits are usually never critically reviewed during the preparation of business cases. In fact, benefit assumptions are often "force fit" in order to make the analysis work. It is very common to find people inflating these estimates in order to come up with financial results that will guarantee their project a speedy approval. And unlike costs, benefits are also more

# FINANCIAL ANALYSIS    *Business Case Part 3.x*

## BENEFIT SUMMARY

|  | Year 1 | Year 2... (through the life of the project) |
|---|---|---|
| Benefit Item A |  |  |
| Benefit Item B |  |  |
| Benefit Item C |  |  |
| Total Added Revenues |  |  |
|  |  |  |
| Benefit Item D |  |  |
| Benefit Item E |  |  |
| Benefit Item F |  |  |
| Benefit Item G |  |  |
| Benefit Item H |  |  |
| Total Cost Reductions |  |  |
|  |  |  |
| Total Benefits |  |  |

*Provide a summary of your project benefit assumptions. It will help
to categorize your benefits where possible as is shown in this example.
Complete the benefit checklists on pages 110-112 for each item, and
include them in the appendix.*

difficult to manage because they are subject to variables that are potentially outside the control of project management.

Benefits assumptions are usually classified into two categories in the Benefits Summary:

- ✧ Added revenues
- ✧ Cost Reductions

The template for the Benefits Summary is shown on page 99 and is completed in a fashion similar to the Cost Summary. You should find that the two categories in the Benefits Summary will capture the nature of most project revenue assumptions. Of course, you should use more appropriate categories if the ones on the template do not apply for your company.

When discussing benefits, it again helps to put on your "banker" hat. If you were lending out your own money, the question you might ask is: "What's in it for me?" In other words, "How much will I earn on my investment (the money I give to the project) to compensate me for the added risk I am assuming and also the length of time my money is tied up?"

Benefits represent inflows of cash to the company or the return generated from the capital given to you by the bankers. Benefit assumptions communicate to your lenders exactly how they will recover their initial investment plus an appropriate rate of return on that investment. The better you are at describing and explaining how your project's benefits will be realized, the better the chance that management will approve your project (i.e. lend you the money). I cannot over emphasize the importance of explaining your project's benefits in terms that convincingly convey to management that your assumptions are of high quality, easily quantifiable and are verifiable once the project is completed.

Similar to the checklists that you filled out for each cost assumption, additional checklists are provided to ensure your benefit assumptions are thoroughly prepared. Before reviewing the checklists, I would like to comment on the quality of the benefit assumptions in general. I have developed two additional quality classifications based on my experience of reviewing benefit assumptions. Surprisingly, the classification technique is not some sophisticated algorithm; the assumptions are simply classified as to whether they are **strong** or *weak* benefit assumptions. This may seem highly subjective and arbitrary, but after several examples it will become quite easy to distinguish between strong and weak benefits. By increasing everyone's awareness as to what constitutes a strong and a weak benefit, the overall quality of your business cases will improve.

You may ask why this distinction is made for benefits and not for costs. This is because benefits tend to be the "creative" part of a project's analysis. And because most companies have no process in place to evaluate projects once they are completed (to see if they delivered as promised), most people may figure, "Who will ever know?" Benefits tend to be overly optimistic, and company accounting systems are usually not sophisticated enough to isolate one project's impact on company sales and operating costs. Project cost assumptions on the other hand are usually easier to track, and many companies have developed project tracking systems to monitor a project's cash disbursements.

## STRONG BENEFITS

A benefit is considered "strong" when one can easily visualize that assumption turning into cash in the company's bank account once the project is implemented. The assumption would also be classified as strong if the company "banker" can easily understand the nature of the cash inflow. "Bankers" desire clear, unequivocal proof that the benefit assumption will ultimately turn into cash. In the real world, however, we all know that nothing is ever that certain. Lenders are always willing to accept some risk, but there is a catch. The payback or rate of return on the project must be higher in order to compensate for the higher level of risk they are willing to accept.

If it was your company, can you visualize the benefit assumptions producing real money that would flow into your pocket? If you cannot, then the assumptions are not considered strong benefits. It is best to look at some examples in order to help understand the different classification of benefits and what makes them strong.

### Strong Benefits – Example 1

New Products or Enhancements of
Existing Products that Increase Sales

In the hopes of gaining new markets for their products many companies are turning to the ever-expanding frontier of the internet. The financial services industry, in particular, is one area that is actively involved in redefining the nature of their customer services, and many banks have spent considerable resources on projects for on-line internet banking. The cost assumptions for these projects are fairly straightforward because building the infrastructure to support internet service is not excessively complex. Developing the benefits assumptions for these business cases becomes the challenge. Benefits could originate from added service charges for subscribers, increased opportunities to cross-sell products or lowering back office and branch support as people move to more automated ways of managing their money.

Venturing onto the internet is still new territory for most companies, and it should come as no surprise that the benefits are subject to considerable risk. Nevertheless, adding a new product to a company's portfolio of products or enhancing the position of an existing product are activities that can lead to the development of strong benefit assumptions. This is not to say that you should accept these assumptions at face value. Appropriate due diligence is required to test their reasonableness.

## Strong Benefits – Example 2

Eliminate or Reduce Current Operating Costs

Another commonly used benefit assumption is the elimination or reduction of a company's current operating cost. These are always considered good assumptions, especially if the cost reductions are readily quantifiable and verifiable. That is, the calculation of the assumption is rather straightforward and the company has a means for validating the results.

Eliminating or reducing operating costs is the category most frequently used by people advocating technology improvement projects. Improving hardware and software systems are always touted as surefire ways to lower ongoing costs. Companies that are highly customer service oriented (such as airlines, insurance companies, and banks) provide good examples of businesses where technology projects can lower operating costs. In these types of businesses it is common to find technology projects such as automated phone answering systems for example, which are used to handle the high volume of customer calls. Although these systems are not cheap, one of the advantages of selecting them is the lowering of labor costs.

Usually any type of automation project would seem to fit into this category. The important point to remember is to scrutinize the assumptions for reasonableness and quality. Your review of these types of projects must focus on delivering the reductions to the bottom line. Be mindful of projects that promise cost reductions in one department but are coincidentally offset by "pressing" needs in other parts of the organization. This is called the "balloon" effect. Like squeezing a balloon, "squeezing" costs out of one area of the company often just shifts them to some other place—no real reduction has occurred.

6

## Strong Benefits – Example 3

### Productivity Improvements

Improving productivity is another favorite area for company projects. Increasing productivity is really just a hybrid of 'Example 1—higher sales' and 'Example 2—lower costs'. The difference, however, is that productivity improvements are targeted at making *existing* systems or processes more efficient. This could involve a combination of higher revenues and lower costs. Assumptions that include productivity improvements could be labeled "strong" benefits if costs are truly driven down and/or sales volumes go up. More often than not, people just say that processes become more efficient, and they calculate a theoretical saving to the company. These assumptions need to be rigorously challenged to see if they pass the "money in your wallet" test.

Earlier in the book an example of a productivity improvement was given for a mass transit system. By improving the transit operation's computer systems, train speeds could increase thereby reducing commuting times. The shorter travel times would entice more commuters to try mass transit, which in turn would contribute to higher revenues. (This assumption must be challenged, of course, to see if the increased passenger levels are reasonable.) Many other valid reasons for improving the computer system could also exist, such as addressing safety issues or acknowledging that the vendor no longer supports the old system. Although the motivations may differ, the results are usually the same: productivity improvements often contribute to higher sales and/or lower costs.

Another example of higher sales and lower costs from productivity is the installation of credit card scanners on the gasoline pumps and islands of many service stations. Once a novelty, credit card scanners and even machines that take cash are removing the need for human interaction when it comes to refueling your car. These devices help increase sales volume by shortening the length of time it takes to refuel. Faster refueling means you can process more cars in the same amount of time. A potential downside to this strategy of shortening your stay at the pump is the reduction in sales of non-gasoline products. Gasoline stations often supplement their traditional petroleum-based products by selling food, lottery tickets, cigarettes and other consumables. A project whose analysis just focuses on the increased throughput at the pumps could overlook some potentially serious impacts to other parts of the business.

---

### Strong Benefits – Example 4

Complying with Government Policy

Although technically not a benefit, sometimes you have to do a project just because the government says so. Mandatory projects could include complying with government regulations regarding environmental protection, disabilities and safety for example. On the surface it may appear there is no quantifiable financial basis for such a project. While this may be true, there should still be a discussion in the business case of the risks of non-compliance. This discussion should include a thorough assessment of the costs avoided by complying with government laws. The costs may be financial such as monetary penalties and non-financial such as negative publicity and a damaged reputation. Of course, you should also discuss the impact on people, the environment or whatever the law was designed to protect in the first place.

Avoiding costs through compliance of government regulations is a slightly different twist to the definition of a strong benefit. And although cost avoidance is highly theoretical in nature, it still provides a valid and substantial reason to do a project.

---

## WEAK BENEFITS

It is more common to find weak benefit assumptions in the business cases of capital projects. What usually makes a benefit weak is the obvious lack of effort taken to thoroughly document and test the assumption—to see if it passes the "money-in-your-wallet" test. As you saw in the previous examples, strong benefits are both quantifiable and verifiable. Weak benefits on 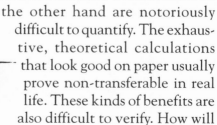 the other hand are notoriously difficult to quantify. The exhaustive, theoretical calculations that look good on paper usually prove non-transferable in real life. These kinds of benefits are also difficult to verify. How will the company know whether they ever realized the benefits? Project sponsors and managers must consider how the company will measure the project to ensure that results are delivered. The following are examples of commonly used weak benefit assumptions.

### Weak Benefits – Example 1

Cost Reductions that Save a Fraction of a Person

I have seen many cases that include a benefit assumption that states:

*"This project will result in workforce
reductions of .5 FTE (full-time equivalent
workers) in the following areas..."*

Unless your workforce is hourly, the odds of this assumption coming true are remote. The fractions of FTEs saved in all the affected areas may add up to a big number and look quite impressive in the financial analysis, but this type of benefit should raise a warning flag. Resist the urge to use, or be leery of, benefits that promise incremental improvements across wide areas of the company. These assumptions usually include statements like:

*"This project allows everybody in
the company to be more efficient"*
or
*"Employees will all have an
extra hour each day to work on..."*

Your business case is very weak if you believe this kind of benefit will result in tangible financial results for the company. If you are still confident, despite the warning that the benefit will produce across-the-company productivity improvements, the responsibility is yours to document a convincing argument that the proposed cash flows are real. Include your argument in the narrative section of your business case if you are not sure whether the company will see monetary benefits but still feel there are worthy intangible benefits. Intangible benefits will probably not get your project approved, but it may provide an important "swing" vote if management has to choose between multiple projects.

### Weak Benefits – Example 2

#### Improved Efficiency but Can't Verify the Savings

The accounts payable department of one company was fed up with the way its employees purchased supplies. The present process was very paper intensive, time consuming and fraught with error. The department developed a project to implement a new credit card program across the company. According to the business case, the benefits were self-evident. Each employee's productivity promised to be greatly improved over the prior, manually intensive method of purchasing supplies. The business case estimated the theoretical hourly savings for one person, annualized those savings and then multiplied them by the 2,500 employees identified as users. The resulting total benefit made the project team look like heroes.

Did this project really save any money for the company? It was very hard to tell. My guess was that the company saved no money because there were not any workforce reductions or additional sales generated by the new program. In fact, the company's costs actually increased because of the project's implementation expenses. Should the project have been approved? In this example, the financial justification would not warrant approving the project. There may have been more valid financial and non-financial assumptions that would make this an easy decision to approve, but the case as presented was very misleading. The big hole in the analysis was understanding what the employees were doing with the time freed up by the improved process. No one really knew. A company cynic would say that these people now had more time to "surf" the internet or play computer games.

There really are no financial benefits if work processes are not rearranged which can ultimately lead to tangible cost savings. As in the first example, sweeping generalizations regarding productivity improvements across the entire company rarely, if ever, lead to real benefits. Management must aggressively challenge productivity assumptions to see if real value is created for the company.

6

### Weak Benefits – Example 3

Cannibalizing the Company's Other Products

Whenever projects involve the development of new products it is quite common to expect some kind of impact on the company's existing product lines. When the Ford Motor Company introduced the sporty *Probe* vehicle into its product lineup some years ago it fully expected there would be some decrease in the sales of its *Mustang* car line. Although these cars were physically very different, they both targeted similar markets.

If your project impacts other product lines in your company in a similar fashion, you should account for the possible reductions in sales of those products as customers switch to the new product. By ignoring the effects of product cannibalization all you are effectively doing is shifting money from one product line to another. No real benefit is derived for the company. The objective of doing a new project is to increase the size of the pie, not rearrange the slices.

### Weak Benefits – Example 4

Synergy Benefits

Synergy benefits are frequently seen in projects supporting acquisitions. They are another potentially classic example of academic theory run amuck if they are not properly developed. In theory, synergy benefits are created by the formation of a collaborative partnership between the parent company and the company being acquired. Because of this partnership, the acquirer can take advantage of the acquiree's knowledge and therefore develop new products and services. As you might have guessed, the theory does not translate well in the real world. Cultural, political and communication issues often surface that quash any hope of a collaborative partnership.

For many analyses, "synergy benefits" are just a fancy name for "unidentified benefits needed to get the project approved." In one case, a corporate team working on an acquisition literally strong-armed its operating divisions to sign up for synergy benefits. Although many of the divisions had little knowledge of the targeted company, they were forced to commit to millions of dollars in projects that had little hope of even making the drawing board. The problem was the company desperately wanted to make the acquisition. Management even had a price in mind before the analysis was completed, and synergy benefits were needed in order to get the project approved. The acquisition did occur, but none of the synergy benefits ever materialized.

Be very leery of any business case that includes synergy benefits or "knowledge transfer" benefits. These types of benefits sound very convincing on paper but in practice are very difficult to deliver. You must be absolutely convinced as to how synergy benefits would be implemented before you include them in your analysis.

**6**

## BENEFIT CHECKLISTS

When it comes to actually quantifying the benefit assumptions, most people always manage to find a way to make the math work. The tough part comes in the verifying stage. How will the company know if they have really captured the benefits? And who is responsible for delivering the benefits? People usually forget to answer these questions. As was done for project costs, benefit checklists are available to help you build a solid foundation for each of your project's benefit assumptions.

Once you have itemized your benefits in the Benefit Summary, you can now proceed to "run" each item through the Benefit Checklists. Just like costs, completing the Benefit Checklists will help you to thoroughly document your case. The checklists contain three parts and are very similar to the ones shown earlier:

> ✧ Description and derivation
> ✧ Accounting treatment
> ✧ Assumption sensitivity section

To repeat, *you should use the checklists for every benefit assumed in the business case*. If you have five benefits, then you will use these checklists *five* times. Include the answers to the checklist questions in the appendix of your business case in case management cares to examine the derivation of the assumptions.

The purpose of the first Benefit Checklist is to thoroughly document the nature of the benefit assumption under review. This includes explaining how the amount and timing were determined as well as who is in control of the benefit. Several items on this checklist (the ones with only a 'yes' option) are mandatory requirements that every project must address.

## Benefits Checklist 1: Description & Derivation

Benefit Item:_____ *(Run each benefit through this checklist)*

| Number | Applies to Project | Review Topic | Guidance/Action |
|--------|--------------------|--------------|-----------------|
| 1 | ❑ Yes | Benefit description | Describe the nature and amount of the benefit in simple terms. |
| 2 | ❑ Yes | Benefit classification<br>❑ New product<br>❑ Product revision or enhancement<br>❑ Cost reduction<br>❑ Productivity improvement<br>❑ New product | Check the applicable box or boxes |
| 3 | ❑ Yes | Benefit calculation | Show and explain the derivation of the benefit estimate (do the math). If the benefit is based on sales projections, did you meet with marketing/ sales to incorporate their input? |
| 4 | ❑ Yes | Timing of benefits | In what time period will the benefit be realized? How was the timing determined? |
| 5 | ❑ ❑ Yes No | Inflation | Have you factored inflation into your benefit assumption? |
| 6 | ❑ Yes | Benefit ownership | Who in the organization is responsible for this assumption? Will this benefit be under the direct control of the project manager or does it involve someone outside of the project's control? |

Benefit Checklist 2 is designed to make you think about how the accounting department handles the benefit once the money is actually received or cost avoided. A key question that must be addressed is "who owns the benefits?"

### Benefits Checklist 2: Accounting Treatment

Benefit Item:_____   *(Run each benefit through this checklist)*

| Number | Applies to Project | Review Topic | Guidance/Action |
|---|---|---|---|
| 1 | ❑ Yes | Measure and verification of benefits | Explain how the benefits will be measured and verified (i.e. How will your "banker" know if the benefit was achieved?) |
| 2 | ❑ ❑ Yes No ❑ Not Required | Accounting consultation | Did you meet with the accounting department to discuss the accounting treatment or did you guess? If yes, with whom did you meet? |
| 3 | ❑ Yes | Posting of benefits | What specific operating area in the company will incur the benefit? Where will the benefit be posted on the general ledger? Is that area aware that this benefit will be assigned to their cost center? Business units outside the sponsoring organization must review and approve any benefits assigned to their area. |

The final Benefit Checklist addresses the issue of preparing a sensitivity analysis around the benefit assumption and is helpful to convey the degree of risk associated with the estimate.

## Benefits Checklist 3: Assumption Sensitivity

Benefit Item:_____ *(Run each benefit through this checklist)*

| Number | Applies to Project | Review Topic | Guidance/Action |
|---|---|---|---|
| 1 | ❏ Yes | Assumption sensitivity | Itemize the things that can cause this assumption to change? Include a discussion of economic risk (i.e. What kind of economic environment is assumed?) and market risk (i.e. What is the risk associated with competition or other market factors?) |
| 2 | ❏ ❏ Yes No | Cannibalization potential | Will this assumption affect any of the company's existing products? |
| 3 | ❏ ❏ Yes No | Benefit control | If this benefit is under the control of an organization external to the project, is there anything that can hinder the obtainment of the benefit? |

Project development involves translating the company's strategic vision into the tactical operations of the company. And project benefits provide the link between the strategic decision making processes (i.e. finding new sources of revenues or cost efficiencies) and the day-to-day operations of the business. If the benefits are properly prepared, the proposed project will integrate smoothly into the company's daily operations. If they are not properly prepared, the organization will struggle with the project's implementation. I cannot emphasize strongly enough the importance of having a benefit section in your business case that is solid and well thought out. Let your case speak for itself that your benefit assumptions are credible and are deliverable. Don't give management the ammunition to shoot holes in your assumptions.

## Contingencies

**N**ever commit to something you cannot deliver is practical advice followed by many a successful manager. Because of this thinking, most people like to build "breathing room" into their assumptions to account for those unforeseen challenges that always seem to occur. If you have never included a contingency in your financial assumptions, then you have probably not worked on project development very long. You may not have an assumption specifically labeled as contingency, but contingencies can take the form of understated benefits or overstated cost assumptions.

How much contingency is enough? There is no one right answer to this question. Risk levels vary greatly from project to project, and establishing a fixed contingency rate (like 10%) is nonsensical. As a matter of practice, you should disclose whatever methodology you are building into your project for contingencies. This disclosure can take the form of specifying a line item in your analysis as "management contingency" or discussing the conservatism of your cost and benefit assumptions.

Some people may not feel comfortable disclosing their contingencies. You may think that if management sees it, they will take it away. Because the corporate cultures of companies are so different on this issue, you will have to make the call. In my opinion the best policy is full, up-front disclosure. Your responses to the *Cost and Benefit Checklists* will provide more than adequate support for justifying a contingency.

As you have seen from the last several sections, building your project's assumptions for benefits and costs are no easy matter. The Benefit and Cost Checklists will help you in your effort to prepare a well-grounded business case. Take the time, and use the checklists for every project assumption. The effort invested in this stage of the process will pay back many fold when it comes approval time. The project management team will also greatly appreciate this effort once the project is implemented. And do not be bashful about asking for help. As stated earlier, project development is a team sport. Consult

### Have You Forgotten Anything?

How do you know you have considered everything in your cost and benefit analyses? Unfortunately the answer is you can't really know for sure. Because organizations are dynamic, changing environmental conditions (be they internal or external) could have a material impact on your project. The Cost and Benefit Checklists were designed with this in mind, and they should help you to minimize the impact of such "surprises." Because of the volatility surrounding projects, it is often wise to include a management contingency in your analysis. (Please refer to the earlier discussion on Contingencies.)

Outside of changing organizational conditions, the main reason that cost and benefit assumptions are mistakenly left out of the analysis is that not enough attention was paid to their initial development. A quick fix is to link the project team members' compensation to project performance. The team must be held accountable for delivering the value shown in the project business case. Once that link is established, the team will make extra sure that every detail is included.

with your company's finance or controller's organizations on the development of any or all of your assumptions. The more people you involve in building your business case, the more buy-in the organization will have on the project.

## INCOME STATEMENT AND CASH FLOWS

The Income Statement and Cash Flows is the very first part of the Financial Analysis section of the business case. The template on page 116 follows a format that most companies use for monitoring financial information. As you can see from the template, it will not be possible for you to fill out this section before completing the cost and benefit analyses. Having finished those analyses, filling out this form becomes rather simple. Insert the itemized benefits and costs, along with their respective financial data, into the Income Statement part of the schedule. The format is very basic and you can decide on the categories for best displaying your data. The categories shown on the template correspond to the advice offered earlier.

## DEPRECIATION

In order to complete the depreciation line of the schedule, you will have to prepare a list of the hardware or other assets that you plan on purchasing. You should have already done this part when you completed the Capital Investment Cost section of the Cost Summary. That list should itemize all the assets you plan to buy and when you plan to buy them. You can have your project's financial analyst prepare the appropriate depreciation schedules for each of those assets, but I strongly recommend that you consult with someone in your company's fixed asset accounting department first. This department is the "keeper of the law" on depreciation schedules.

Depreciation is a relatively straightforward cost to calculate, and it would be easy for me to give you the formulas for preparing your own schedules. The problem with doing that, however, is that each company has its own unique way of calculating depreciation for the assets it purchases. Don't do extra work by trying to prepare your own depreciation schedules. You would also only be guessing on the proper accounting treatment. Go right to the source and have accounting provide you with the correct figures. Consulting with accounting saves you the work of estimating depreciation yourself, and it also

# FINANCIAL ANALYSIS    *Business Case Part 3.x*

## INCOME STATEMENT AND CASH FLOWS

|  | Year 0 | Year 1 | Year 2... |
|---|---|---|---|
| **INCOME STATEMENT** | | | (through the life of the project) |
| Project Benefits | | | |
|   Added Revenues | | | |
|   Cost Reductions | | | |
|   **Total Benefits** | | | |
| Project Costs | | | |
|   Implementation | | | |
|   Other... | | | |
|   **Total Costs** | | | |
| Depreciation of Investment | | | |
| **Profit Before Taxes** | | | |
| Taxes @ ____% | | | |
| **Profit After Taxes** | | | |
| CASH FLOW ADJUSTMENTS | | | |
| Capital Investment | | | |
| ImplementationCosts | | | |
|   (Capitalized) | | | |
| Add Back Non-Cash Items | | | |
| **Cash Flow** | | | |

## EVALUATION OF CASH FLOWS

|  | Project Results | Company Requirement |
|---|---|---|
| IRR | ____% | ____% |
| NPV(Discounted at ___%) | $_____ | $_____ |
| Payback | Between year ____ and year ____ | Between year____ and year____ |

makes accounting part of the project team. Should the accounting group not provide the depreciation in a timely manner, tell them you will estimate it yourself and that you will highlight in the business case that accounting was contacted but refused to help. That will get their attention. I'm sure you will find that that tactic will not be necessary; most accounting functions are eager to please. Additional information on depreciation (which I highly recommend you read) is included in Appendix 6 of this book.

**6**

## TAXES

Determining the taxes is the final step in completing the Income Statement. Completing the tax line on the Income Statement is easy to do if you know the proper tax rate to use. Like depreciation, tax is an area that you should not attempt to figure out by yourself. Obtain the proper tax rate from your finance department or someone in tax accounting. Addressing tax issues for your project is simply not limited to the one line on the Income Statement. Appendix 7 highlights other areas in the financial analysis that are affected by taxes. Because taxes take such a big "bite" out of profits, this is an important area for you to review.

## CASH FLOW

Once the Income Statement is completed, the attention now turns to calculating the project's cash flow. Cash flow is defined as the actual movement of money into or out of the project. It is not concerned with the promises that companies make or receive, such as the promises to pay bills (accounts payable) or the promises to receive payment for goods sold (accounts receivable). Companies that record those promises are said to be keeping their financial books on an accrual basis. The Income Statement that was just prepared represents an accrual basis of accounting, which is what management is accustomed to seeing when it reviews the company's financial data. It is important to display the project's information this way because it shows management how the project will ultimately impact the company's financial statements.

There are also a few situations where the decision to approve the project is based on how the company's income statement is affected, but that is rare. Almost all projects are judged on cash flow. This is particularly true in smaller companies where cash resources may be somewhat constrained. Determining a project's cash flow is not tremendously difficult as is reflected by the following formula:

> **Benefits**
> - **Costs**
> - **Depreciation**
> - **Taxes**
> = **Profit After Taxes**
>
> + **Non-cash costs**
> - **Capital Investment**
> = **Cash Flow**

Adding back non-cash costs and subtracting capital investment costs from the Profit After Taxes calculated in the Income Statement will produce the proper cash flow values for the project. Determining the non-cash costs should be relatively straightforward for your project's financial analyst. Depreciation is an example of a non-cash cost because it represents the cost of an asset spread over its useful life. In any given year, depreciation does not reflect the actual cost that was paid for the asset. Since depreciation is factored into the Income Statement (as a cost that lowers the Profit After Tax), adding it back in the cash flow calculation basically cancels it out. The example that follows shows a completed Income Statement and Cash Flow schedule. This schedule clearly demonstrates how depreciation is netted to zero in the determination of the project cash flows.

## EVALUATION OF CASH FLOWS

Once your cash flow projections are complete, you must now determine whether your project is financially attractive. There are many different ways to analyze cash flow. The methods that are most commonly used include payback, return on investment (ROI), net present value (NPV), and internal rate of return (IRR). Of course, there are more sophisticated approaches. But the discussion here will

| | Year 0 | Year 1 | Year 2 | Year 3 | Year 4 | Year 5 | Total |
|---|---|---|---|---|---|---|---|
| **INCOME STAEMENT** | | | | | | | |
| Project Benefits | | | | | | | |
| Added Revenues | | $10 | $60 | $110 | $160 | $210 | $550 |
| Cost Reductions | | 80 | 80 | 80 | 180 | 180 | 600 |
| Productivity Gains | | 10 | 10 | 10 | 10 | 10 | 50 |
| Total Benefits | | $100 | $150 | $200 | $350 | $400 | $1,200 |
| Projected Costs | | | | | | | |
| Implementation Costs (Expensed) | | (100) | | | | | (100) |
| Total Costs | | ($100) | $0 | $0 | $0 | $0 | ($100) |
| Depreciation of Capital Costs | | ($110) | ($110) | ($110) | ($110) | ($110) | ($550) |
| Incremental Profit Before Taxes | | ($110) | $40 | $90 | $240 | $290 | $550 |
| Taxes @ 38% | | (41) | 15 | 34 | 91 | 110 | 209 |
| **Profit After Taxes** | | **($69)** | **$25** | **$56** | **$149** | **$180** | **$341** |
| **CASH FLOW ADJUSTMENTS** | | | | | | | |
| Capital Investment | ($500) | $0 | $0 | $0 | $0 | $0 | ($500) |
| Implementation Costs (Capitalized) | (50) | 0 | 0 | 0 | 0 | 0 | (50) |
| Add back non-cash costs (Depreciation) | 0 | 110 | 110 | 110 | 110 | 110 | 550 |
| **Cash Flow** | **($550)** | **$41** | **$135** | **$166** | **$259** | **$290** | **$341** |

6

strive for a more balanced approach by focusing on methods that are both financially sound and can be readily understood and accepted by the organization. I will review the strengths and weaknesses of the different methods used for evaluating financial data and will provide some helpful tips on important things to keep in mind as you prepare your analysis.

No matter what methods are selected (NPV, IRR, payback, etc.), companies must first establish financial thresholds for determining whether the evaluation results are acceptable. Financial evaluations by themselves are meaningless. For example, a company may set a policy that a project's payback must be less than two years and its IRR must be greater than 15% in order for it to get approved. Chances are your company has already determined the hurdle rate or levels that projects must clear. Check with your finance department to obtain these values.

One commonly used hurdle is called the cost of capital. The cost of capital is uniquely derived for each company, and it is the key "measuring stick" against which all projects are judged. Appendix 8 provides additional information on how this most important measure is derived. Do not attempt to calculate the cost of capital yourself. You will have to obtain this value from your finance department in order for you to complete the financial evaluations that follow.

## When You Need to Have More Power

There are many different ways to evaluate cash flow. Some methods are quite simple and some are very sophisticated. Some companies stick with the simplest of approaches while others use complex financial and statistical theory such as the Black-Scholes option formula. My experience has shown that those companies with high research and development spending usually require greater analytical horsepower. Because the outcome of research and development projects is highly uncertain, statistical modeling can give companies

greater insight on probable outcomes before big
money is spent on the project.

Of course, using more complex analytical
methods generally involves hiring higher-skilled
financial analysts and buying additional computing
power and modeling tools. Select a more complex
approach if your company requires it, and you believe
your company is capable of understanding the
theory. Companies that require (or desire) more
sophisticated approaches should consult other
finance reference material for greater insight into
statistical theory.

**6**

DECISION ANALYSIS EXPERTS TRYING TO FIGURE OUT
WHERE TO GO FOR LUNCH

## PAYBACK

Determining the payback period for a project is the easiest of the evaluation methods to calculate. The payback period represents the length of time it takes for the project to break even or recover its initial investment. The simplicity of this method makes it one of the most widely used evaluation techniques in project analysis. Despite its popularity, payback has serious drawbacks if it were the only method used for ranking projects.

There are two approaches used for calculating payback, the regular method and the discounted method. The regular method is the most commonly used approach, but it has a significant shortcoming. It fails to account for the time value of money (i.e. a dollar today is worth more than a dollar tomorrow). The discounted method is similar to the regular method except the net cash flows are discounted by the project's cost of capital.

The payback period is a measure of liquidity because it lets you know how long your money will be tied up. All things being equal, projects with shorter payback periods are more attractive. This method can also provide you with a rough estimate of the project's risk because longer payback periods are inherently riskier. The further the cash flows are pushed into the future, the greater the risk that something might affect them. Projects with shorter payback periods are considered less risky because there is less time for things to go wrong. The following example illustrates how payback is determined. All cash flows are assumed to occur at the end of the period.

### EXAMPLE 1: REGULAR PAYBACK METHOD

| | Initial Project Cost | Year 1 | Year 2 | Year 3 | Payback |
|---|---|---|---|---|---|
| **Project 1** Cash Flows | ($100,000) | $100,000 | $0 | $0 | |
| Cumulative Cash Flow | ($100,000) | $0 | $0 | $0 | By end of year 1 |
| **Project 2** Cash Flows | ($100,000) | $50,000 | $65,000 | $100,000 | |
| Cumulative Cash Flow | ($100,000) | ($50,000) | $15,000 | $115,000 | Between years 1 |
| **Project 3** Cash Flows | ($100,000) | $10,000 | $10,000 | $300,000 | |
| Cumulative Cash Flow | ($100,000) | ($90,000) | ($80,000) | $220,000 | Between years 2 |

Some people like to build false precision into their payback analysis by carrying out the calculations to one or more decimal places. Determining the month the project breaks even is not possible when annual cash flows are used. Unless monthly cash flows are available, it is of no value to say that project 2's payback is 1.72 years. It is best to simply say the project pays back between its first and second year.

6

The example shows why using payback as the only evaluating criteria is dangerous. Imagine that you are the manager that has to pick one of the three projects, and payback is the only evaluation methodology you will use. Your assistant, knowing that you are very busy, spares you the details of the cash flows and prepares a nice executive summary of the three projects:

### Executive Summary

**Payback Period**

|  |  |
|---|---|
| **Project 1** | Less than 1 year |
| **Project 2** | Between year 1 and year 2 |
| **Project 3** | Between year 2 and year 3 |

Based on the executive summary, you might select project 1 although it just breaks even and earns nothing more. Only the third project stands to earn more for the company. Example 2 looks at the same three projects but uses discounted payback. All cash flows are assumed to occur at the end of the period and are discounted at a cost of capital of 10%.

## EXAMPLE 2: DISCOUNTED PAYBACK METHOD

Cost of Capital = 10%

| | Initial Project Cost | Year 1 | Year 2 | Year 3 | Payback |
|---|---|---|---|---|---|
| **Project 1** Actual Cash Flows | ($100,000) | $100,000 | $0 | $0 | |
| Discounted Cash Flow | ($100,000) | $90,909 | $0 | $0 | |
| Cumulative Discounted Cash Flow | ($100,000) | ($9,091) | ($9,091) | ($9,091) | None |
| | | | | | |
| **Project 2** Cash Flows | ($100,000) | $50,000 | $65,000 | $100,000 | |
| Discounted Cash Flow | ($100,000) | $45,455 | $53,719 | $75,131 | |
| Cumulative Discounted Cash Flow | ($100,000) | ($54,545) | ($826) | $74,305 | Between years 2 & |
| | | | | | |
| **Project 3** Cash Flows | ($100,000) | $10,000 | $10,000 | $300,000 | |
| Discounted Cash Flow | ($100,000) | $9,091 | $8,264 | $225,394 | |
| Cumulative Discounted Cash Flow | ($100,000) | ($90,909) | ($82,645) | $142,749 | Between years 2 & |

There are significant differences when using the discounted payback approach. A new executive summary might show:

### Executive Summary

| | Regular Payback | Discounted Payback |
|---|---|---|
| Project 1 | Less than 1 year | No payback |
| Project 2 | Between year 1 and 2 | Between year 2 and 3 |
| Project 3 | Between year 2 and 3 | Between year 2 and 3 |

Project 1 no longer breaks even and the payback for project 2 is pushed into the following year. The payback period is not sufficient information by itself to decide on a project's worthiness. You must have additional information on the project's cash flows. As shown in example 2, project 3 clearly adds more value to the company.

Many companies set payback thresholds such as "all projects must payback within two years." Although these may seem arbitrary, there are circumstances when setting such a policy makes sense. Suppose you were the owner of a company that you planned to sell in two years. Would it make sense to fund projects that did not payback within the two-year time frame? Unless the project's long-term value got factored into the sales price, there is no reason to give your money away.

The simplicity of the payback method makes it a valuable piece of information in the approval process. It is especially helpful when used in conjunction with other evaluation techniques but can be very misleading if used by itself.

## RETURN ON INVESTMENT (ROI)

Perhaps one of the most important measures that shareholders use to determine the effectiveness of their investment is return on equity or ROE. ROE measures how much is earned on the stock-holders' equity investment in the company. Return on investment or ROI is very similar. ROI measures how much is earned on the company's capital that is invested in the project. There are many different ways to calculate ROI, and it is always best to define the components of ROI whenever you use it.

Two commonly used definitions of ROI are:

1. $ROI_1 = \dfrac{\text{Average project net income}}{\text{Average project investment}}$

2. $ROI_2 = \dfrac{\text{Average project net income}}{\text{Initial project investment}}$

$ROI_2$ uses the initial project investment in the denominator and makes no attempt to account for the differing levels of investment over the project's life. ROI is a very simplified way of measuring project performance, and its biggest benefit is that management readily understands it. Its major drawback, however, is that it does not account for the time value of money. You can, of course, modify the equation by using discounted cash flow in the numerator.

As mentioned earlier, ROI is not a universally embraced measure like payback or net present value. Its definition is highly variable. If you use ROI make it a point to communicate its definition through-out your company, and strive to consistently apply it. *Always* include a description of how the ROI is calculated whenever you state it for a project. Stating the definition will eliminate any potential confusion associated with a measure that has many different interpretations.

## NET PRESENT VALUE (NPV)

Net present value or NPV is the preferred method for evaluating projects because it takes into account the time value of money and the cost of the money used to fund the project. NPV is calculated by discounting a project's cash flows by the project's cost of capital. Discounting the cash flows means finding how much the future cash flows are worth in today's dollars. As was discussed earlier, the cost of capital is the discount rate used to help make this calculation. Net present value includes the term "net" because some of the cash flows can represent outflows (e.g. capital investments, expenses) or inflows (e.g. benefits). The present value of each cash flow is simply netted together. Although NPV is not a complex method, many people still have difficulty understanding the concept. The following example should help explain why the measure is effective.

### Example

Suppose a long-lost uncle died and left you an inheritance of $500,000. Right after you deposit the money in your bank account, you receive a telephone call from your cousin Vinny, the stockbroker wannabe. Vinny heard of your good fortune and is most concerned that you have access to some good financial advice. Because he would like to help you, he offers to manage your investment. And because you are "family," Vinny offers to waive his customary advisory fee. Vinny proposes a five-year investment strategy. He guarantees that you will receive $15,000 for each of the five years and at the end of the five years you can choose to get your initial money back or have Vinny reinvest it again.

### Is this a good deal?

In order to answer this question you must first determine the cost of capital for your inheritance. The cost of capital in this case represents an opportunity cost, which is the rate you can earn on your money if Vinny was not available. (You can read more about opportunity costs in Appendix 5.) After a little research, you may decide that the best alternative is to invest your money in United States Treasury five-year notes. The yield on these notes, say 5% in this example, represents the opportunity cost of capital you would use to evaluate Vinny's proposal.

You prepare the analysis as follows:

| Initial Investment | Year 1 | Year 2 | Year 3 | Year 4 | Year 5 |
|---|---|---|---|---|---|
| ($500,000) | $15,000 3% | $15,000 | $15,000 | $15,000 | $515,000 |
| Outflow from you | Inflow to you | Inflow to you | Inflow to you | Inflow to you | Inflow and return on investment to you |
| Discount rate | 5% | | | | |
| NPV | ($43,295) *[Calculate using a financial calculator or spreadsheet software progam—there is no need to use present value tables anymore!]* | | | | |

6

## How should you interpret the results?

NPV < 0   Projects with negative NPVs have cash flows that are not sufficient to repay the invested capital or the cost of that capital. At a given cost of capital, projects with negative NPVs destroy shareholder value. ***Avoid investing in these projects.***

NPV = 0   If the NPV equals zero, the cash flows are just sufficient to repay the invested capital and provide the required rate of return on that capital. Projects with zero NPVs do not destroy nor create additional shareholder value. In these circumstances, shareholders are indifferent to projects with NPVs equal to zero. The odds of actually getting zero are infinitesimal. If your NPV does equal zero, check that someone did not input zero into a spreadsheet cell that should have been calculated.

NPV > 0   An NPV greater than zero represents a project that truly adds value to the shareholder. These kinds of projects provide a return in excess of the shareholder's cost of capital requirement. ***Shareholders will support projects with positive NPVs.***

SHOULDN'T BE HARD TO SEE THAT 3%
PAYMENTS ARE LESS THAN THE 5% ALTERNATIVE
DUH!

You should not accept Vinny's investment advice because his proposal resulted in a negative NPV of $43,295. Kindly thank him and invest your money in U.S. Treasury notes or find an investment strategy with an even better NPV. NPV is a very powerful measure for evaluating capital projects. Be sure to *always* state the discount rate assumption that you are using whenever you calculate the NPV of a series of cash flows. NPV is a meaningless number if there is no stated discount rate.

## INTERNAL RATE OF RETURN (IRR)

The internal rate of return or IRR is one of the most widely used measures for evaluating projects in business today. Corporate managers actually prefer this measure to NPV because the answer is conceptually easier to understand. Saying a project has an internal rate of return of 20% seems to have more impact than saying the project has an NPV of $5,000. People are also more comfortable working with percentage-based calculations. We are all accustomed to using rates of return everyday on such things as personal investments (stocks, bonds, savings accounts) and debt (home and automobile loans).

The internal rate of return on a project is the return one would expect to earn on the project's capital investment. This number only makes sense when it is compared to the cost of capital. If the IRR is greater than the cost of capital, shareholder value is created. If the IRR is less than the cost of capital, shareholder value is destroyed. If the IRR equals the cost of capital, the project's cash inflows are sufficient to cover its investment costs and the financing charge for using the company's funds. In other words, the IRR represents the rate at which the present value of the project's investment costs (or initial cash outflows) equals the present value of the project's benefits (or cash inflows).

**Present value (Investment costs) = Present value (Cash Inflows)**

Let us return to the example in the previous section and calculate the IRR for Vinny's proposal. (You will need a financial calculator or spreadsheet program in order to calculate IRR.) The proposal produces an IRR of 3% which means that Vinny's promise to pay you

$15,000 per year for five years equates to earning only 3% on your initial $500,000 investment. This is not a good plan since you have a perfectly acceptable alternative investment that would give you a 5% rate of return. The alternative investment is even more attractive because you consider it to be significantly lower risk than dealing with your cousin. When given a choice, the objective is always to select the investment that yields the greatest rate of return for the lowest risk. This applies equally to personal and business situations.

Is IRR a better measure than NPV since it is so widely embraced by management? Academically speaking, IRR is not considered as good a measure as NPV because there are circumstances where you may get conflicting results. Shareholders are primarily interested in selecting projects that create the most value, and NPV specifically calculates how much value (in monetary terms) is created by the project. It is possible that some projects could have large IRRs but small NPVs. You might not select the project that provides the greatest wealth to the shareholder if you were to only focus on IRR. This frequently occurs when comparing projects of unequal size.

## Example

Suppose you have two projects, and you can only select one. Assume that both projects are of equal risk, and your cost of capital is 10%. The project cash flows are as follows:

|  | Initial Investment | Year 1 | Year 2 | Year 3 |
|---|---|---|---|---|
| Project 1 | ($100,000) | $20,000 | $20,000 | $120,000 |
| Project 2 | ($10,000) | $2,500 | $2,500 | $12,500 |

The calculations for each project's NPV and IRR are as follows:

|  | NPV | IRR |
|---|---|---|
| Project 1 | $24,869 | 20% |
| Project 2 | $3,730 | 25% |

Note: Cost of Capital = 10%

If you just used IRR to make your selection, you would select project 2 because its rate of return is 25% versus 20% for project 1. Is this the best decision for the shareholder? If you used NPV to make the decision, you would select project 1 because its NPV of $24,869 far exceeds the NPV of project 2. Although project 2 has a higher rate of return, you would have to implement it many times over to equal the same value created by project 1. Given a cost of capital of 10%, you should select project 1 because it adds more value. Granted the size of the capital investments in this example are quite different, and you may say the example is slanted, the point is that you should strive to select projects that add the greatest wealth to the shareholder when comparing projects of unequal size.

Another potential problem area for IRR is projects that have non-normal cash flows. A project is considered "normal" if its cash flows fit the general profile:

| | Initial Investment | Year 1 | Year 2 | Year 3... |
|---|---|---|---|---|
| Normal | (outflow) | + inflow | + inflow | + inflow |

A project's cash flows are considered "non-normal" if there are cash outflows in the later years.

| | Initial Investment | Year 1 | Year 2 | Year 3... |
|---|---|---|---|---|
| Non-normal | (outflow) | + inflow | + inflow | (outflow) |

Projects with non-normal cash flows can cause problems such as multiple IRRs or errors in the IRR calculation. You can use NPV or a modified version of IRR in these cases to determine the project's rate of return.

### Modified IRR

The modified internal rate of return or MIRR actually produces a better answer than IRR because MIRR assumes that the project's cash inflows are reinvested at the cost of capital rate. IRR on the other hand assumes that the project's cash inflows are reinvested at the project's own IRR. The best way to explain MIRR is by displaying a project's cash flows on a timeline as demonstrated using project 1 from the earlier example.

## Example

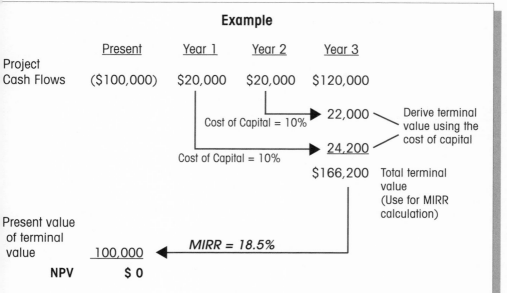

| | Present | Year 1 | Year 2 | Year 3 |
|---|---|---|---|---|

Project Cash Flows ($100,000) $20,000 $20,000 $120,000

Cost of Capital = 10% → 22,000 — Derive terminal value using the cost of capital

Cost of Capital = 10% → 24,200

$166,200   Total terminal value (Use for MIRR calculation)

Present value of terminal value   100,000 ◄— MIRR = 18.5%

**NPV**   $ 0

The cash inflows occurring in year 1 and year 2 are reinvested at the company's cost of capital (10% in our example). (Imagine that you are putting the cash from the project in a savings account that pays 10%.) Since this project only lasts three years the first year's cash inflow can be reinvested for two additional years, and the third year's cash inflow can be reinvested for one additional year. The resulting values at the end of year 3 are called the project's terminal value. The project's terminal value of $166,200 is used to calculate the MIRR.

| | Initial Investment | Year 1 | Year 2 | Year 3 |
|---|---|---|---|---|
| Project 1 | ($100,000) | $ 0 | $ 0 | $166,200 |

The IRR calculated for project 1 was 20% as compared to the MIRR of 18.5%. MIRR provides a more accurate determination of the rate of return for a project, and it is especially valuable when projects exhibit non-normal cash flow patterns. MIRR's biggest drawback, however, is that it is very complex to explain. Odds are high that you will lose your audience's attention (and possibly your own) the moment you draw the above timeline. Consult with your finance department to see if MIRR should be included in the business case. Because it is very easy to calculate MIRR using a spreadsheet, I recommend that it be calculated along with the standard measures of payback, NPV and IRR.

IRR is definitely a more intuitive measure although there are situations when its use is not appropriate. In these circumstances it is best to use MIRR or NPV. Overall, IRR is a very powerful evaluation tool that provides management with a quick, understandable

## What About EVA™?

The financial evaluation measures covered in this chapter are the ones that are used most often by companies today. One approach not reviewed that seems quite popular is economic value added or EVA™. (EVA™ is a trademark of Stern Stewart & Company.) Although the calculation methods differ, EVA™ and net present value both lead to the same answer. One of the many reported benefits of using EVA™ is the creation of a better linkage between capital project analysis and operational performance management. In other words, the measurement method used to evaluate capital projects is the same one used to evaluate how you run the business on a day-to-day basis.

There are many supporters of the EVA™ approach. Its greatest challenge, however, is that it requires a cultural shift in the company's financial management strategy. And as many people know, changing a company's culture is a much greater challenge than one might initially anticipate. The total approach to EVA™, including linking it into the compensation strategy, is impressive and worthy of consideration if you feel your company is capable of making such a major shift in thinking. If your company already uses EVA™, you will find that this book's approach to project analysis is entirely compatible. Simply insert your EVA™ calculations in the financial analysis section instead of using the traditional cash flow evaluation techniques. The emphasis on developing quality business and financial assumptions through this process applies no matter what evaluation method you choose.

assessment of a project's worthiness. Project analysis is especially enhanced when IRR is used in conjunction with NPV.

We have reviewed several different analytical techniques in this section:

- ✧ Payback
- ✧ Return on investment
- ✧ Net present value
- ✧ Internal rate of return
- ✧ Modified internal rate of return

These five measures represent by no means an all-inclusive listing of the methods companies employ to evaluate capital projects. There may be other methods that you consider more appropriate for your business. It is best to not rely on just one measure because each has its own unique strengths and weaknesses. Using multiple methods should not pose an added analytical burden since most people use computer spreadsheets to prepare their financial projections. It should be fairly easy to program your spreadsheet to calculate all of these items. Of course, the answer to most of these measures will only make sense if you know your company's expectations for acceptable performance. Assuming you know your company's financial thresholds for getting projects approved, you now must interpret the data. Does your financial analysis make any sense?

## INTERPRETING THE DATA

You have done a considerable amount of work so far if you have followed all of the recommendations for building your business case. You have:

- ✓ Analyzed your business requirements and alternatives
- ✓ Built detailed cost and benefit assumptions
- ✓ Consulted with your company's accounting and business experts to validate and test your assumptions
- ✓ Analyzed your financial projections using some or all of the evaluation techniques described in the previous section
- ✓ Obtained your company's approval criteria to compare against your project

Now you must determine if your financial results make any sense. How will you know if the results are reasonable?

It is always helpful to prepare a summary of the results whenever you complete an evaluation of your cash flow projections. Be sure to include your company's expectations for the project in that summary. The example that follows uses the format shown in the Evaluation of Cash Flow section, which is included in the template on page 116.

### Project Evaluation Summary

|  | Project Results | Company Requirements |
|---|---|---|
| NPV | $50,000 | > $0 |
| IRR | 18% | > 12% |
| Payback | Between years 2 and 3 | < 4 years |

Project results that fall short of your company's requirements will force you to re-examine the derivation of your cost and benefit assumptions. Because people have invested a lot of personal time in the project so far, there is a tendency to go back and modify the assumptions to produce an answer that management wants to see. Be very leery of following this strategy. "Sugar coating" or artificially boosting your financial performance most likely will come back to haunt you. Remember that management will expect you to deliver on any promises that you make. You may be setting yourself up for a fall if there is no substantive plan to deliver on your higher projections. On the other hand, there may be a valid reason for your project's poor financial performance. Other overriding, non-financial business reasons, like environmental compliance or safety, may justify doing the project. The business analysis section in your business case can justify the project in these cases.

Projects with obscenely high rates of return are no cause for celebration either. Most people generally subscribe to the bigger is better school of management, but proposing a project with an astronomical rate of return warrants a visit by the financial analysis "police." I have seen actual proposals where managers swear that their projects will deliver internal rates of return of greater than 100%. Although it is not impossible to achieve such results, it is just highly unlikely. In such cases, the project's costs are probably grossly understated and/or the benefits are overstated. After reviewing such incredible projections, don't be surprised if you find management asking, "If our company historically has a rate of return of 15%, how is it that your project can deliver 100%?" You and your project will become quite popular if your analysis is correct because management will want to invest more money in projects like yours.

Surely you must think that if the project produces results close to the company's expectations everything would be all right. An additional review of your assumptions is also warranted in these situations, although the nature of the review is different than the prior two cases. Management will be more interested in understanding the sensitivity of the assumptions. Sensitivity analysis basically seeks to answer the question: "What can go wrong with the project?" Management will want to understand the volatility of the assumptions and under what circumstances the project becomes undesirable.

As was repeatedly said in the previous sections, you must have some kind of benchmark data to compare against your project's results in order to see if they make sense. The company requirements provide one source for comparison, but there are others. You might want to research similar projects in your company to understand how they performed against the company requirements. Also, many projects often have the option of being outsourced versus being built in house. In these cases, it is likely that external benchmarking data is available. No matter what benchmark you end up selecting, determining whether your data makes sense always requires that you re-examine the thoroughness and accuracy of your assumptions.

## IMPACT TO BUDGET (LINKING THE PROJECT TO THE BUDGET PROCESS)

One of the biggest disconnects that occurs in companies is having a capital spending process that is poorly linked (or not linked at all) to the ongoing operational budgeting process. People will often develop their annual expense budgets thinking that they have included everything, or they have developed them at such a high level that they could not possibly account for incremental projects. Only later, after the project is approved, does the manager realize there is no money set-aside in the annual budget. This section provides some background on operating and capital budgeting, and it also discusses ways to ensure your project is not a "surprise" to the budget. Or if it is a surprise to the budget, senior management will be well informed *before* the project gets approved.

Why should anyone care whether the annual budget includes a provision for capital projects? Conceptually, one might argue that it should not matter whether the project is in the budget or not. If incremental projects truly add value to the company, the right economic decision is to raise the capital to fund as many projects as the organization is capable of supporting. The focus of the annual budget should remain on the day-to-day operational matters and not be concerned with long-term capital projects.

There are two fundamental ways of looking at capital budgeting. One approach is to assume there is an unlimited supply of capital. If your project is in the best economic interest of the shareholder, the company will raise the necessary capital to fund the work. The other approach assumes there is a limited supply of capital where you are forced to compete against other projects for a finite pool of resources. The latter approach is the one most companies follow, and it comes from a principle most of us have grown up with—there is only so much money to go around. The odds for manipulating or "gaming" the process greatly increase in this environment because the limited approach forces people to intentionally manipulate the analysis in order to show their projects in the most-favored light possible. Limited capital forces managers to put aside conservative estimates because they know their "safer" financial projections cannot compete against the more aggressive, higher-risk estimates given by other projects. In this type of environment, over selling the idea is the ticket to project approval.

The limited approach was most likely born from an overall lack of accountability in the capital budgeting process. Because management was accustomed to project managers over promising and not producing what shareholders expected, they reacted in a seemingly logical manner—protect the resources that you have and only give them out to the highest bidder. In other words, the less I give out, the less I have to lose should the projects that are funded not deliver as promised. While the "capital is unlimited" approach may seem more enlightened, it will only work if there is a process in place for holding project managers and sponsors accountable for delivering results.

Monitoring operational budgets is very similar to the limited supply of capital approach just described. Normally, you are allocated a limited "pot" of money and your performance on how well you spend it is tracked on a monthly basis. Because managers in most companies are under intense pressure to make or better their operating budgets, they may hesitate to undertake additional work unless it improves their short-term budget performance. It therefore becomes critical to proactively address these concerns in the project's business case. If the project is not in the budget, then management needs to approve the project knowing that. Unless specifically told, management will most likely assume the project is in *somebody's* budget. It is best to resolve this issue up front before any money is spent.

6

> If your project is approved after your budget was finalized, you can be sure that management will want to know how your project impacts the budget.

How do you know if your project is in the budget? At a training class at one large company, I had the opportunity to ask project managers this question and to explain the importance of documenting their project's impact to the company budget. Not one of the fifteen managers could say whether their project was accounted for in their budgets. Determining whether your project is in the budget is a very difficult question to answer for most managers because they are often not directly responsible for preparing the budget.

If you are responsible for preparing the business case for your project, it becomes your responsibility to contact the analyst who developed your area's budget. You will have to work with that individual to understand whether the budget assumptions include your project. The following template on page 138 will help explain your

# FINANCIAL ANALYSIS    *Business Case Part 3.x*

## IMPACT TO BUDGET

|  | Project Dollars Included In | | |
| --- | --- | --- | --- |
|  | Business Case | Approved Budget | Variance |
| Capital | $ | | |
| Benefits | $ | | |
| Expense | $ | | |

Explanation of Variance

Capital:


Benefits:


Expense:


*List the reasons for each variance. If only part of the project is budgeted, explain why. If none of the project is budgeted, explain why it was not included. Also include a discussion of how any negative variances will be overcome.*

project's impact to the budget.

The format shown in the template is meant to provide a high-level financial summary of the differences between the approved budget and the business case. Discuss any differences in the explanation of variance section on the template. If the variances are bad (i.e. your approved budget is less than your project's values), you should consult with the Finance organization and discuss ways that these variances can be overcome. Include a summary of that discussion in the template.

Identifying the project's impact to the budget is a mandatory section in the business case. Including this section clearly demonstrates to management that you understand how your project fits into the other key financial processes within the company. Preparing this section is relatively easy if you can find the individual who prepared your area's operating budget. That person should readily know whether the project was accounted for in the revenue, expense and capital budgets of your operating group.

## FINANCIAL ATTESTATION

The Financial Attestation section of the Financial Analysis will come as a surprise to most people who have prepared business cases because one typically associates financial attestation with auditors reviewing the company's financial statements. Auditors provide an independent review of the company's books and offer reasonable assurance that the financial data conforms with generally accepted accounting principles. While it is not necessary to go to that extreme (using an independent auditor for an individual project), it would be tremendously beneficial for companies to apply a hybrid of this activity to business case preparation.

An independent review of the financial data could uncover weaknesses in the business case assumptions. It would also give management a little more piece of mind as to the integrity of the case. But whom would you get to do the attestation? I recommend that your company identify a handful of your top financial analysts and make reviewing business cases an additional responsibility. This should not be their only responsibility, however. Choose enough analysts so the additional work doesn't negatively impact their primary duties.

# FINANCIAL ANALYSIS  *Business Case Part 3.x*

## FINANCIAL ATTESTATION

❑ Financial analysis acceptable; estimates are conservative
❑ Financial analysis acceptable; estimates are not conservative
❑ Financial analysis marginal; exceptions are noted below
❑ Other (Explain)


Exceptions
<u>Item</u>                                    <u>Responsible Individual</u>


Signature

_____          _____
Financial Analyst Reviewing the Case          Date
Analyst's Business Area

*Assign a financial analyst not directly connected with the project to review the financial analysis including the assumptions behind the cost and benefit analysis. Note any exceptions and have the analyst sign and date the form.*

An analyst should also not be connected in any way with the project being reviewed. And to be sure an analyst doesn't review the same group's projects all the time, the business cases should be selected randomly so that each analyst gets to review a good cross-section from the company. This additional step need not add a lot of time to the overall process. The independent reviewer can provide feedback to the analyst preparing the financial assumptions as the project's financial analysis is being developed.

The template for the Financial Attestation is shown on page 140. The reviewing analyst should note any exceptions to the derivation of the cost and benefit assumptions, as well as the financial evaluation, and who will be responsible for taking corrective action if any is required.

**6**

Reviewing business cases and attesting to their reasonableness can be a very high profile assignment for a financial analyst. Pick your best analysts for this responsibility so it is seen as recognition of superior performance. And just to get the analyst more committed to the process, tell them that in the event that something were to go wrong with the project, they will be responsible for conducting a thorough post-project review. This process may seem like extra work, but I think you will find that senior management will welcome the idea. It also benefits the finance community because it makes them more involved in the company's capital project process.

## SUMMARY

As demonstrated by the variety of the subject matter and the length of the topics, the Financial Analysis chapter is easily the most complex part of this book. The chapter began by reviewing the importance of preparing a good financial analysis and then led us through discussions on developing meaningful assumptions, evaluating the data to see if it is reasonable, and finally understanding the project's impact on the company's budgeting process.

The primary goals of this section were to present material that would allow the reader to:

✔ Prepare a thorough financial analysis based on sound financial theory

✔ Improve the effectiveness and efficiency of your analytical process by following easy-to-use, structured templates

✔ Present the material in a convincing manner that management will readily approve

If you are successful in achieving these goals, you have greatly improved the odds of success for your project. The recommendations outlined in this chapter, once implemented, will help establish greater controls on the company's analytical process with the end result being an improvement in the project's exposure to risk. Although the financial analysis is now complete, our attention remains focused on ways to better understand and manage the things that can go wrong with the project. The next chapter provides guidance on preparing a high-level sensitivity analysis for your project.

❖

6

> "It takes a very unusual mind to undertake the analysis of the obvious."
> — ALFRED NORTH WHITEHEAD

## TOP-FIVE CRITICAL DRIVERS

*What are the top-five mission critical drivers for this project? (The project would not succeed if these five things were not done right.)*

## SENSITIVITY ANALYSIS

Include a brief discussion of the potential risk to the project in the following areas:

> Economic Risk
>
> Schedule Risk
>
> Market Risk
>
> Technology Risk
>
> Government/Regulatory Risk
>
> Other

*Modify these categories to suit your particular business situation. Include any assumption checklists in the appendix.*

# WHAT CAN GO WRONG?

O ne can never completely eliminate project risk. We can make efforts to minimize it, however, and to communicate better the risk that remains. One of the objectives of this book is to provide a process that ensures that quality time is spent on business and financial analysis so companies can make more intelligent decisions on where to allocate resources. Selecting projects with the highest return and lowest risk profiles is easier if a thorough risk assessment is included in each business case.

Preparing the project's overall risk assessment is the focus of the 'What Can Go Wrong?' analysis. This analysis involves examining every assumption in the business case as well as the environmental factors affecting the project. As each element is reviewed you literally must ask, "What can go wrong with that assumption?" When finished, the 'What Can Go Wrong?' section should give the reader a sense of the risk inherent in the project assumptions.

The material in this chapter expands on the assumption sensitivity checklists included in the earlier discussion on costs and benefits. The individual checklists from those sections and the one in this chapter should provide you with sufficient information to complete the 'What Can Go Wrong?' section in the formal business case.

The What Can Go Wrong? Template on page 144 includes two sections:

✦ Top-five critical drivers

✦ Sensitivity analysis

## TOP-FIVE CRITICAL DRIVERS

The top-five critical drivers asks you to list the five most important things that would have to be done right or the project would not succeed. This could include things that are necessary in order to keep your project's promised delivery date or it could include the support of a key operating area within the company. As an example, a company implementing a new systems solution for its sales team might have a critical driver that says:

> *The project must receive support as scheduled from the network engineers in the Information Technology group. Failure to adhere to the schedule may cause the project to be delayed subsequently impacting the sales team just as it enters the peak-selling season.*

Highlighting the key areas that are necessary to ensure a project's success will give management a "heads up" so resources can be properly prioritized. Listing the top-five drivers is also good for the project manager and sponsor because it will enable them to focus on the things that are most important. The next chapter on Impact Analysis will go into more detail as to how you can ensure that your project receives the support it needs.

## SENSITIVITY ANALYSIS (WHAT CAN GO WRONG? CHECKLIST)

Managing and minimizing the company's exposure to risk is one of management's primary responsibilities. In order to fulfill this responsibility larger companies may have dedicated risk management functions or controls in place to better manage the riskier parts of the business. Project managers can do their part to address these concerns by proactively analyzing their project's exposure to risk and by communicating the degree of variability that is possible in the project's outcome. The sensitivity analysis section asks you to review some of the more macro-level concepts of risk that may be facing your project, such as economic, market and technology risk. The following checklist provides guidance on how you can complete this section of the business case. Keep your answers brief, and feel free to expand the checklist to account for the unique risk profile of your company.

## What Can Go Wrong?

**7**

| Number | Applies to Project | Review Topic | Guidance/Action |
|--------|--------------------|--------------|-----------------|
| 1 | ❏ Yes | Benefit and cost assumptions | Determine the top-five critical benefit and cost drivers. |
| 2 | ❏ Yes ❏ No | Economic risk | Is the project sensitive to changing economic conditions? What kind of economic environment is assumed—low growth, high growth? |
| 3 | ❏ Yes ❏ No | Schedule risk | What is the probability that the project will be completed on time? |
| 4 | ❏ Yes ❏ No | Market/ competitive risk | How sensitive is the project to competitive forces? Are there any risks associated with price changes or changes in buyer behavior or demographics? |
| 5 | ❏ Yes ❏ No | Foreign/political risk | Are there any political events or issues that could affect the project? (e.g. building a new facility could be opposed by local civic groups) Is the project subject to foreign political risk if international markets are involved? Is the project sensitive to foreign exchange rate fluctuations? |
| 6 | ❏ Yes ❏ No | Government/ regulatory risk | Are there any legislative or regulatory factors that could affect the project? Consider governmental impacts from federal, city, state or provincial sources. (e.g. environmental regulation might mandate certain project specifications) |
| 7 | ❏ Yes ❏ No | Technology Risk | Does the project utilize equipment that is subject to technological obsolescence? |

## Qualitative vs. Quantitative

Since projects all have different risk profiles it would be ideal if one could classify projects according to their degree of difficulty, similar to the classifying of events in the competitive sports of diving and figure skating. Unlike the repetitive routines of diving and skating, however, quantifying risk is extremely difficult in practice because projects are rarely ever the same. The sensitivity analysis should therefore start out as a qualitative discussion, but it does not have to be limited to that. Some companies have designed very complex statistical models that can quantify financial risk, but this modeling is only possible if the company has maintained a good database of historical project performance. Even though most companies do not possess good databases on project performance, a quality sensitivity analysis is still possible if you focus on the potential variability of each assumption. One can always develop different scenarios by modeling the key assumptions that are sensitive to external or internal drivers. For example, projects may yield different financial results depending on the external economic conditions that are assumed. A poor economic scenario may force a project to lower its revenue assumptions and subsequently its financial return to shareholders.

## Get Real

Most people prepare business cases that present only the "best-case" scenario to management. You are not doing yourself any favors by painting such an optimistic picture. Without an understanding and appreciation of the risk inherent in the project, management will assume that your best case projection is easy to deliver. The degree to which you aggressively challenge your own assumptions will send a strong, positive message to management that you are focused on the company's bottom line. Senior management will recognize those project managers who are truly objective and spend the time to uncover potential weaknesses in their projects.

*i.e- "TRUST"*

## IMPACT ON OTHER DEPARTMENTS
*Discuss what departments are affected by or are needed to support the project. Also discuss **how** these departments are impacted.*

## IMPACT ON OTHER PROJECTS
*Discuss if this project impacts any other projects that may be ongoing in the company.*

## IMPACT ON EXTERNAL GROUPS
*Discuss if there is an impact to any groups outside the company.*

# IMPACT ANALYSIS – DEVELOPING SUPPORT FOR YOUR PROJECT

Project Development is a team sport. As basketball superstar Michael Jordan says, individual contributors are important, but it takes the combined efforts of the entire team to deliver the big prize. How can you ensure that all the members of the team are in alignment with the objectives of the project? The only way to guarantee alignment with the project's goals is to gain the total support of every member on the project team. This chapter will focus on the often-overlooked members of the team who are needed to make your project successful. The recommendations in this section will help you to:

> "Talent wins games, but teamwork and intelligence win championships."
> – MICHAEL JORDAN

✧ Identify the key people, organizations or projects that may be impacted by the project

✧ Increase the level of awareness of the project within the impacted areas

✧ Obtain the full support of the affected area managers **before** the project is implemented

Impact Analysis identifies those key players who are not part of the project's sponsoring organization but whose operations are either affected by the project or are needed to support the project. We are primarily interested in the groups outside of the sponsoring organization because these are the areas where one usually experiences difficulties with conflicting priorities. Individuals who belong to the sponsoring department normally have work priorities that are better aligned with the project. This is because sponsoring management tends to have a deeper understanding of the project's importance and therefore has a vested interest that their team member's work schedules are properly prioritized. Team members who do not belong to the sponsoring organization face greater management challenges. These individuals, whose time is not 100% dedicated to the project, usually end up reporting to two bosses—one from their home organization and the other from the project team. This dual reporting relationship is the primary cause of many problems. Team members often must struggle with conflicting priorities that result in the project not getting the right amount of support at the right time. "I'm just too busy" or "I'll get to it" are frequently heard responses to requests for assistance. The approach as outlined in this chapter will free you from the typical 'deli-counter' response where a key support area asks you to take a number and patiently wait your turn.

As you identify the parties that are potentially impacted by the project, have a sheet of summary information on the project available to share. Many people do not see the need to provide such written documentation. Instead, they believe a simple telephone call is all that is required. It is very important that you document any interactions with the impacted areas. This written confirmation could be very beneficial later on—especially if people fail to recall the details of earlier telephone conversations when commitments are often made. Put your requirements in writing, and get the impacted area's buy-in early in the project's design stage.

## PROJECT NOTIFICATION TEMPLATE

The Project Notification template (shown on pages 154 and 155) is designed to provide a summary look at the proposed project. It includes a brief discussion of the project's purpose, its expected timing and a high-level implementation plan. There is also a listing of the operating areas potentially impacted by the project as well as sections to provide feedback. You will use this form during your discussions with the impacted area managers.

The organizations that are needed to support the project will greatly appreciate the information provided in the Project Notification template. Creating this information page and having a follow-on meeting with the impacted area manager are simple acts that will generate considerable goodwill between the departments. All too often project managers fail to gain the necessary buy-in before projects gets started. Most of us can personally relate to or imagine the consequences of such actions. Giving someone little or no notice that their support is required is the fastest way to generate resentment between operating areas. The Project Notification template will keep you from alienating the key operating groups that are needed to make the project successful.

Once completed, the Project Notification template essentially becomes a marketing brochure for the project. Your task then is to determine the areas in the company that require notification. Use Section 7 of the notification sheet to list the functions and organizations you believe are needed to support the project. Target these areas for distributing the information sheet and then arrange the necessary meetings to gain support. Before you meet with the managers of the impacted areas, note your expectations of the work their areas need to provide in section 8 of the template. As you prepare your expectations, leave some additional space for the impacted area manager to provide feedback or other ideas that you may have overlooked. Section 9 is also provided to ascertain whether there are other areas in the company that were mistakenly omitted or not considered in Section 7. Many project managers may feel they know how their project impacts the company, but you will see that reviewing the Project Notification template is an effective and efficient way to validate their thinking. As you finish your discussion with the impacted area managers, document any follow-up assignments or meetings that were agreed upon. You should also ask the manager to formally acknowledge receiving the project notification by signing the notification sheet.

# PROJECT NOTIFICATION TEMPLATE

1. Project Name:


2. Project Sponsor:


3. Project Manager:


4. Impacted Area Being Contacted:
*Identify the area that is receiving this information.*


5. Project Purpose:
*Briefly state the reason(s) you are doing the project.*


6. Implementation Plan:
*Include a high-level discussion of the work plan including the anticipated scheduling of the project.*

## 7. Key Support Functions Required to Support the Project:
*List all of the areas that are not part of the project's sponsoring organization (the area listed in #2 above) that are required to support the project.*

<u>Function</u>          <u>Organization</u>               <u>Contact Person (if known)</u>

## 8. Support Required From Impacted Area:
*Describe the support you need from the area (listed in #4 above) that is reviewing this information sheet. Leave space for them to input information that the project team may have overlooked.*

## 9. Additional Support Required:
*Have the impacted area manager list any other groups that he/she may know of that were not included in section7 but should be included.*

## 10. Follow Up Required:
*Note if you agreed to any follow-up work or meetings. Include due dates of any deliverables.*

## 11. Project Acknowledgment:
*Have the impacted area manager sign and date this page to acknowledge the formal notification of the project.*

_____          _____
Name, Title, Organization, Date          Name, Title, Organization, Date

The information requested in the Project Notification template is meant to be fairly high level and easy to put together. Perhaps the biggest challenge you will encounter is determining all of the areas that are potentially affected by the project. To overcome this challenge it helps to classify the impacted areas into three groups:

1.  Other departments within the company that are not part of the sponsoring organization but are needed to complete the project

2.  Other projects within the company

3.  Groups outside of the company

## IMPACT ON OTHER DEPARTMENTS

This section refers to recognizing those departments outside of the sponsoring organization (but still within the company) that are needed to complete the project. As mentioned earlier, there may be members of the project team who effectively have two bosses—one from their home department and the other from the project team. The conflicting priorities experienced by these team members often become a major contributor to project delays and overruns. You can avoid these consequences by defining the project requirements up-front and securing the support you need from the impacted areas.

It may be hard to identify all of the impacted departments at first so consider examining the functions that are needed instead. Once the functions are identified it should be fairly easy to find the department in the company that provides the service. It is helpful to think of the functional needs according to the following categories:

✧ **Designers** – people who are needed to support the design stage of the project

✧ **Builders** – people who are needed to implement the project once it is approved

✧ **Operators** – people who will provide the ongoing support to the project after the implementation phase is completed

✧ **Users** – people who are the clients of the product or service the project produces

These functional groupings can provide you with a good starting place for organizing the project team. As you identify the organizations that provide the functions needed for your project, the Project Notification template can help facilitate any discussions you will have with the managers of those support areas. Include a brief discussion of how your project impacts other departments (including the nature of the support required) in the first section on the Impact Analysis template on page 150.

## IMPACT ON OTHER PROJECTS

Large companies may have hundreds of different project implementations underway at any given time. Whether your company is implementing a hundred projects or just two, you should consider whether your project has the potential to impact other efforts that are in progress within the company. It is always important to have a good understanding of the relationship between projects when the work of one project may depend upon the successful completion of another. A very simplified example will help illustrate this point.

Suppose you are the manager of a large landscape architecture firm that was just awarded a major contract for landscaping the city's biggest community park. This is an extremely important and strategic contract for your company because of its high profile. You are concerned that everything go just right because any difficulties could directly impact future business. The contract stipulates that your firm install new lawn areas, extensive tree plantings, and numerous flower arrangements. Unfortunately there is one complication. The city public works department awarded a separate contract to another firm for the water sprinkler installation. The success of your landscaping project is now directly linked to the successful completion of another firm's work. If you do not integrate the key elements of the other project into the design of your project, you run the risk of implementing a beautiful landscape design that is not supported by the irrigation system. Your company may experience financial losses and a damaged reputation should the new plantings fail because of insufficient watering.

As most of us know, projects are never completely isolated to just one part of the organization. Although the previous example is simple, it highlights that our work world is more interdependent than independent. Interdependencies within the company demand that you analyze how your project impacts other operating areas. The Project Notification template can help you become more aware of how your project interrelates to other parts of the business. As you review your material with the impacted area managers, ask them if they are aware of any other projects that could be affected by your project. Contact the project managers of any potentially conflicting projects that are brought to your attention. Include a brief write-up on any possible impacts on other projects in the Impact Analysis template.

## IMPACT ON EXTERNAL GROUPS

The final section on the template addresses the project's impact on groups outside of the company. It is not uncommon for projects to impact outside organizations such as environmental, political or governmental groups. Few projects will probably fall into this classification, but all it takes is one mishandled communication to result in a public relations nightmare for the company. Maintaining good working relationships with outside organizations is very important, and you must always exercise caution. Review any communication plans with senior management before initiating contact with an external group. Maintaining a good public image is a top priority with most companies, so be sure to follow the proper protocol for dealing with the public.

If you must contact an external party, your company will probably want to prepare an information sheet that is more politically correct than the one you are using internally. Although it may be time consuming and burdensome to clear the administrative hurdles, the goal is to avoid making the small and seemingly innocent comment that can damage the company's public image. Make sure any interaction with public groups is well planned and approved by senior management. Most companies have public relations functions that can assist you with developing and coordinating the strategy for communicating with external groups.

Project managers rarely get all the support they ideally would like. There is an alternative, however, to just complaining if you are one of those managers who continually gets short-changed on the support needed from other operating areas. You can secure the commitments needed for your project by following the process outlined in this chapter. Obtaining impact area support during your project's design stage will most certainly improve the odds for a smoother implementation phase. Although the impacted areas may only play a small role in your project, they are still an important part of the team. Teamwork and intelligence work just as well for ensuring successful projects as they do for winning basketball championships.

❖

**8**

## APPROVAL HIERARCHY
*Provide an organizational view of the project approval hierarchy. Also include any areas impacted by the project.*

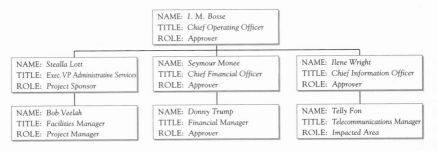

## PROJECT TEAM
*Provide an organizational view of the project team.*

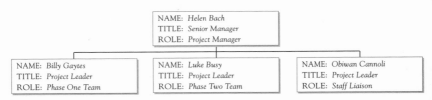

## PROJECT MANAGER
*Include a brief description of the project manager's qualifications.*

## TEAM MEMBER QUALIFICATIONS
*Include a brief description of the qualifications of each of the team members if they are known at the time the proposal is prepared. If you do not know the team members, you may wish to discuss the qualifications of the roles you desire to fill.*

# PROJECT MANAGEMENT

U nlike business case development, there is no shortage of information on how to manage a project once it is approved. Books, seminars and software are readily available to educate us on the finer art of project management. This chapter makes no attempt to offer a preferred method for managing projects. Instead, I recommend that you follow your company's approved approach or consult some other source for additional guidance, if necessary. The purpose of the Project Management section in the business case is to provide a very high-level overview of your project management strategy. Specifically, this section should include a discussion of who has to approve the project, who is on the project team, and finally the expected timeline for the project (see templates on pages 160 and 168). Failure to include these items in the business case is tantamount to asking management for a blank check to fund the project.

## APPROVAL HIERARCHY

'Who has to approve the project?' is a question frequently asked during business case development. Since the answer to this question is company specific, it will become necessary for you to wipe the dust off of your company's policy manual and to find the section on capital spending authorization levels. If you don't want to get dirty, you can always locate the individual in your company responsible for maintaining the policy manual. This responsibility is typically assigned to the corporate secretary's area but may also be in the finance or human resources groups.

As stated earlier, it pays to know the rules before you submit your project for approval. Find out who has to approve the project well before you have to submit the business case, and start lobbying those individuals for support. All of the individuals required to approve the project should be fully knowledgeable of the project *before* the business case crosses their desk. The project approval section in the business case is basically provided 'for your information' and is most effective when displayed in a graphical manner. This section will remove any doubt as to who must sign the final document.

## PROJECT TEAM / PROJECT MANAGER

The work you have done in the previous chapter on impact analysis will definitely help you in determining the composition of the project team. The feedback received from the discussions with the impacted areas should provide some excellent ideas regarding potential players to include in your project's starting lineup. Use the following Team Member templates to summarize the support needed for your project. The information gathered from these templates can then be used for completing the first three parts of the Project Management template (page 160). Place the completed Team Member templates in your business case's appendix.

If you do not know who will manage the project, design the project or build the project, simply note that the positions are not yet filled. In these cases, it might be wise to list your recommended candidates and when you expect to fill the positions. Presenting a business case without an identified project team is not a good strategy but one that is, unfortunately, frequently practiced. My experience has shown that people spend far more time planning their equipment purchases than on determining who should be on the project team. Imagine if you employed that strategy as the coach of a football team. Is your focus before the big game on uniforms and equipment or is it on the players?

## PROJECT MANAGEMENT
## TEAM MEMBER TEMPLATE

9

### Project Manager

Name:
Business Area:
Percent of Time Dedicated to Support the Project
    Required:                    Availability:
Prior Project Management Experience:

*The project manager is responsible for consolidating the business case, steering it through the approval process, implementing the project, providing status reports, and issuing a project completion report once the work is finished.*

### Project Designer

Name:
Business Area:
Percent of Time Dedicated to Support the Project
    Required:                    Availability:
Prior Project Design Experience:
Project Design Tools Required:

*The project designers are responsible for preparing the conceptual design of the project. Similar to the architect developing the blueprints for a building, these individuals are the idea generators. The number of people involved with this task will vary, of course, with the complexity of the project.*

## PROJECT MANAGEMENT
## TEAM MEMBER TEMPLATE (continued)

### Project Builders

Name:
Business Area:
Function Being Performed:
Percent of Time Dedicated to Support the Project
     Required:          Availability:

*The project builders are the people who will implement the project once it is approved. Try to be as specific as possible when listing the functional requirements needed to support the project. It is highly likely that some of the people mentioned in the design section will also be used for building the project.*

### Project Operators

Name:
Business Area:
Function Being Performed:
Percent of Time Dedicated to Support the Project
     Required:          Availability:

*The operators are the people who will provide the ongoing support **after** the project is completed. Most business cases fail to mention the ongoing support needed to maintain whatever it is the project is trying to accomplish.*

## PROJECT MANAGEMENT
## TEAM MEMBER TEMPLATE (continued)

**9**

## Project Users

Business Area:
Representative to Contact:
Product or Service Received from Project:

*Provide a listing of the clients who will receive the products or services the project will produce. Identifying the primary contacts to keep informed of the project's progress is a key element of an effective communication strategy.*

## Project Training

Name:
Business Area:
Type of Training:  ❑ Pre-implementation
                   ❑ Post-implementation
                   ❑ Other _____

*Identify the individuals who will provide training to the end users or project team.*

## PROJECT MANAGEMENT
## TEAM MEMBER TEMPLATE (continued)

### Project Tracking

Name:
Business Area:
Other Responsibilities Required:

*Identify the individual responsible for tracking the project finances and preparing status reports.*

**Prepared by:**

**Date**

The Project Management section provides you the opportunity to preview your project's starting lineup with senior management. I believe that including this often-overlooked section in your business case will demonstrate that your project is better organized than most other projects. Discussing the composition of the team also addresses another major concern of management, which is identifying the individuals to hold accountable for delivering on the project's promises. The project team will benefit as well because the case now documents, for the record, the resources that are required to complete the project.

9

## PROJECT TIMETABLE

I am continually amazed at how often completion dates are omitted from business cases submitted for approval. Not mentioning the completion date or simply putting 'to be determined' sends the message that you are not in control of the project. If you were the project approver, would you write a check to a person who has no idea when they will deliver the product? The purpose of providing your project timetable in the business case is to give management a feel for how long it will take to complete the project. I am not suggesting here that you create a detailed project plan that itemizes the hundreds of actions required for implementation. The timetable for your business case should remain at a very high level and be consistent with the business and financial assumptions used in the case.

Do not send the wrong message to the project approvers by neglecting to complete this simple and straightforward part of the business case. This should be a fairly easy section to put together if you have done a quality job on your financial projections. Like the approval hierarchy, the project timetable is another section that is best presented in a graphical manner. Include on the template on page 168 the start and completion dates at a minimum and any significant milestone dates if they are known.

# PROJECT MANAGEMENT   *Business Case Part 6.x*

## TIMETABLE

*Develop a high-level timetable that can convey significant tasks that are
anticipated in the project. Include a separate line for each major activity or
milestone of the project (if they are known).*

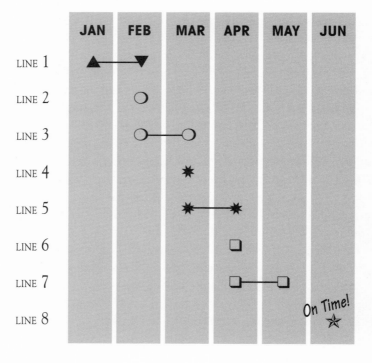

## NAVIGATING THE RAPIDS

Not to sound pessimistic but a lot of things can certainly go wrong between the first task of a project and its last. Many will agree that one of the strongest predictors of a successful project is the project manager's ability to work through conflict. Veteran project managers know their projects are going to experience problems. The project leadership may change halfway into the work plan, or they may experience difficulty finding the right people for the implementation phase. They might also find that other higher-priority assignments are borrowing their resources thereby causing project delays. This book has continually stressed the importance of documenting the project's business and financial assumptions, and that advice applies to project management assumptions as well. You will stand a much better chance of navigating the rapids of difficult times if *all* of your project assumptions are thoroughly documented.

The Project Management section of your business case is designed to help you document:

⋄ The people you will need to get the job done

⋄ Who said it was all right to get started

⋄ When you anticipate finishing the work

Of course, this section can only be developed using information that is available at the time the business case is prepared. The many unknowns that exist at this time can provide an easy excuse for overlooking this section. Do not let that happen to your project. Imagine for a moment that you are building a house, and you are in need of a construction loan. What do you think the banker would say if you told her that you had a general idea of what you wanted to build but had no idea who was going to build it or how long it would take? She would tell you to take your business elsewhere. You are going to have to make some assumptions in your application if you want the banker to approve your loan. Getting your project approved is no different.

Providing the Project Management overview is an integral step in completing the business case because it lets management know who will be spending their money and for how long.

9

**Item:** *State the item being reviewed*
(e.g. Tax rate calculation)

**Definition:** *Describe the item; give the formula if necessary*
(e.g. ROI = Average Profit After Taxes/Average
 Project Investment)

**Results:** *Show the result of the calculation*
(e.g. IRR = 25%)

## Additional Information:

*Show the actual calculation of the result if a complex formula is used.*
*Remove any source of doubt as to how the numbers are generated.*

(e.g. WACC = (After Tax Cost of Debt * Percentage of Debt Used)

+ (Cost of Preferred Stock * Percentage of Preferred Used)

+ (Cost of Equity * Percentage of Equity Used)

= (10% * 30%) + (12% * 10%) + (15% * 60%)

= 13.2% )

## Areas Consulted:

*List the key contacts you consulted in preparing the assumption or analysis.*
(e.g. Seymour Monee, Assistant Treasurer consulted on the
 derivation of the cost of capital)

# BUSINESS CASE APPENDIX

The appendix provides the perfect place for including any backup material that was created (or needs to be created) in support of sections two through six of the business case. Providing this additional information will greatly benefit the business case reviewers should they ever have any questions or desire to "drill-down" into the detail. The information placed into the appendix will also be of considerable help to the project team. If conditions ever were to change and the team was forced to ask management for supplemental funding, project management will be glad they had prepared such a thoroughly documented business case.

The template shown on page 172 is the general format that is recommended for providing backup information for non-checklist items. The template is very basic and easy to complete. It asks for the name of the item being reviewed, how it is defined, what the results of the calculation are (if applicable), additional information (such as showing the actual calculation), and if you consulted with anyone. Using a consistent format for non-checklist items will greatly speed up the review process because the reviewers will quickly get accustomed to the standardized presentation format.

## WHAT TO INCLUDE

Include any additional material that you feel supports the analyses presented in the business case, but be careful not go overboard here. A business case is not like a college term paper—a thicker package does not translate into a higher score by the reviewers. "Bulking" up a document may have worked in school, but it is not perceived well by management. In general, the appendix should have the following items:

- ✔ The completed checklists
  - ✦ Cost
  - ✦ Benefit
  - ✦ What Can Go Wrong?

- ✔ Calculations supporting the financial evaluation
  - ✦ NPV
  - ✦ IRR
  - ✦ Payback...
- ✔ A glossary of project terms
- ✔ An alternative comparison matrix (if applicable)

Once you have completed the checklists, no additional work is required. You may simply add them, as is, to the appendix. For the financial evaluations, use the template to explain the derivation of each measure used in evaluating your financial data. The glossary of project terms is an often-overlooked item, but it is very important. Be sure to include any terms that you feel management may not understand as they read the business case. It is very common for projects (especially technology projects) to use a lot of acronyms, and it is unrealistic to expect that management will know every technical term. Don't make them have to ask you for the secret decoder ring that explains your presentation. The alternative comparison matrix is something most companies create when they have to decide between two or more alternative courses of action. A classic example is a company that has to choose between two different software vendors. The matrix can document the decision criteria that were considered and how each alternative scored. The project team typically determines what the decision criteria are, however, it is not uncommon to find these criteria dictated by someone at the corporate level. The comparison matrix can take many forms, so don't feel constrained by what is shown in the abbreviated example.

**10**

## Alternative Matrix – An Example

| Evaluation Category | Decision Criteria | Weighting | Score (1–4) Choice A | Score (1–4) Choice B | Wtd Score Choice A | Wtd Score Choice B |
|---|---|---|---|---|---|---|
| Technology | – Ability to customize program | 8% | 4 | 3 | .32 | .24 |
| | – Graphical user interface | 8% | 3 | 3 | .24 | .24 |
| | – Adaptable to present network | 8% | 4 | 3 | .32 | .24 |
| | – Meets corporate security standards | 8% | 3 | 2 | .24 | .16 |
| | – Internet capable | 10% | 4 | 4 | .40 | .40 |
| | – Data management | 8% | 3 | 3 | .24 | .24 |
| | | 50% | | | 1.76 | 1.52 |
| Support | – Training requirements | 10% | 3 | 4 | .30 | .40 |
| | – Documentation | | | | | |
| | – Administration | 5% | 3 | 3 | .15 | .15 |
| | – End-user | 5% | 3 | 3 | .15 | .15 |
| | – Change management | 5% | 4 | 3 | .20 | .15 |
| | | 25% | | | .80 | .85 |
| Operational | – Desktop reporting features | 10% | 4 | 3 | .40 | .30 |
| | – Support 24-hour environment | 15% | 4 | 3 | .60 | .45 |
| | | 25% | | | 1.00 | .75 |
| | **Total** | 100% | | | 3.56 | 3.12 |

Completing the appendix marks the culmination of a great deal of work. If you have faithfully adhered to the guidelines presented in this book, your business case will be of the utmost quality. Not only will you have greatly improved the odds of gaining senior management approval, you will also have done your project team a big favor by thoroughly documenting the project's starting assumptions. The next chapter will review some of the finer points of getting your project approved.

# GETTING YOUR
# PROJECT APPROVED

I n the television series, *Star Trek – The Next Generation*, there was a brief yet very effective phrase the captain would always say in order to convey approval of a crew member's recommended course of action for solving some major problem. '*Make it so*' was very powerful because it conveyed the confidence and trust the captain had in the crewmember's proposal. Now that your proposal is complete, how do you get **your** captain to say 'make it so'? This chapter will provide some ideas on how to successfully get your project through the company's approval process.

## POLITICS, POLITICS, POLITICS

The approval process is the stage in the project development life cycle where the project team typically experiences the frustrations of company politics. Knowing how to 'manage your management' becomes a critical skill for gaining the approvals that will launch your project into the implementation stage. Having a thoroughly prepared business case, as was developed following the guidance from the preceding chapters, will take you about 90% of the way toward final approval. The remaining step requires gaining a critical mass of management endorsements that will literally force the final approver to concur with the overwhelming show of support displayed by the

177

company's management team. Getting management buy-in is always more difficult than it sounds, however, because it requires dealing with people's egos.

## Bob, The Know-it-all

At one time or another everyone has worked for a boss who thinks he knows everything. At one company, a senior officer always made it a point to inform his audience that he knew the ultimate right answer on any and every issue. Now this behavior was not to be confused with simply having a strong opinion on a subject. No matter what you were talking about, work or pleasure, Bob was the expert on the subject. People would always joke before meeting with Bob that no matter how brilliant the idea, Bob would tell you a better approach or point out some critical error in your thinking. I think we all know when someone steps over the line of confident knowledge to boastful ego building. And most people also know that this type of management style will keep the workforce from developing the creative solutions to problems that could propel a company forward. Developing projects in such an environment is not very fulfilling, but we come to accept it as a fact of company life.

11

It is definitely not fair to stereotype that all managers possess insecure and egocentric behavioral qualities. There are a great many managers who are very secure and comfortable in their positions and are good at giving credit where credit is due. Working for a boss like this is a real treat because the team becomes the focus of attention. Unfortunately these kinds of people are few and far between so knowing how to deal with highly successful and headstrong managers (the creators and perpetuators of office politics) becomes an important part of getting the project approved.

## KNOW THE RULES

The first place to start in the approval process is gaining a good understanding of your company's policies and procedures. The weaker senior managers will always default to the "work is not in the required format" response when they do not have any substantive feedback to offer. As was discussed in an earlier chapter, it would be very wise to do some research on your company's rules for approving capital projects *before* the business case is finished. Does your company have established guidelines for preparing business case documents? Do not put yourself in the position of having your work summarily rejected because it does not follow the approved format. Do your homework and determine what is permissible. The process described in this book is easily adaptable to any company policy.

You should also investigate your company's approval hierarchy for project funding. This information is usually referenced in a corporate policy that is controlled by a high-level organization like the Corporate Secretary. The approval section (see Example 1) that you include in your business case's Executive Summary should agree with the company's formally approved chain of command for authorizing projects.

---

### Example 1
### Capital Spending Authorization Limits

| Approval Level | Project Spending Limits |
|---|---|
| Board of Directors | Greater than $1 million |
| Chief Executive Officer or Chief Operating Officer | $500,000 – $1 million |
| Senior Vice President | Up to $500,000 |
| Business Area Manager | Up to $250,000 |
| Business Area Supervisor | Up to $50,000 |

Another important piece of information for gaining rapid approval is understanding the company's expectations on the lead time required for submitting proposals. Many companies have very rigid timelines for submitting capital project requests to senior management.

---

**Example 2**

Projects requiring approval by the Board of Directors should use the following schedule for planning purposes:

| Action | Submission Requirements |
|---|---|
| Board Approval | Second week of every quarter |
| Chief Executive Officer Approval | 2 weeks prior to final approval |
| Chief Financial Officer and Finance Staff Approval | 3 weeks prior to final approval |
| Local Area Approval | 4 weeks prior to final approval |

---

In the second example, the project must clear several hurdles prior to the final board of directors' approval. This approval sequence will most likely vary for your organization, but you should anticipate building sufficient lead-time into your project work plan. The bigger the project, the more lead time people will want for analysis and review. Practically speaking, the approval process becomes mostly ceremonial as the project clears the more demanding lower-level hurdles and moves higher up in the approval chain of command.

## GETTING THE BUY-IN

In addition to addressing the company's formal chain of command for capital approval, it is important to acknowledge those operating areas outside the project's host organization that are key to the project's success (refer to the Executive Summary template on page 70). Including the endorsement of the impacted area managers definitely helps to build a level of solidarity around the project. Each approver will consider themselves a member of the project team because they were given a vote. This simple act will reward you handsomely once the project begins requesting support from these areas. Displaying the operating area manager's approval of the project will help to remove any barriers to success once the implementation is underway. Senior management will also be impressed by your thoroughness to obtain buy-in from any key organization that is impacted by the project.

One of the things that you can do to help make the actual step of "signing on the dotted line" a non-event is to identify the project's approvers very early in the proposal development stage. You need to start lobbying the approvers right from the beginning when the concept is first born. Do not wait until the proposal is finished to begin your campaign. Let the approvers know what you are doing, and keep them informed of the project's progress. Also let them know that you will expect their concurrence once the proposal is finished. Very brief executive summaries will work wonders for keeping these individuals abreast of the developing proposal.

Another important point is to always thank the approvers anytime they or one of their staff do something to support the project. Most of us take such support for granted, and acknowledging people is usually given a low priority in our work schedule. We come to expect cooperation as just part of the job. Getting people to work together toward a common goal is what project development is all about so make it a point to continually acknowledge the fine work of your team. The little effort required to do this will pay you back many fold. Keeping the approvers in the information loop during the proposal development stage will all but guarantee your project a rapid endorsement.

Another thing that you can do to put the "seal of approval" on your project is to involve the internal auditing function in the proposal development and approval process. Many internal auditing departments are trying to change the mission of their function from that of a policing activity to one of a highly valued consultant. These groups are seeking a more proactive role in analyzing and developing controls during the design stage of critical functions as compared to the traditional 'what-did-you-do-wrong?' method of auditing. Tell your internal auditing department that you are proposing a project and that you would like their assistance from a *'controls'* perspective. Ask them for a quick assessment. The better internal auditing functions are prepared to give you meaningful advice on potential control issues that may affect your project.

## OTHER THINGS TO CONSIDER

Another potentially creative idea that was mentioned earlier but is worth repeating is to have someone in the finance group give an attestation on the project's financial projections. "Do the numbers make any sense?" is a question that is usually asked whenever a case is presented for approval. Consider having a skilled and independent financial analyst review the financial assumptions in order to give an opinion of the financial health of the project, just as an outside auditor would provide. You do not have to get an analyst from outside the company, just pick an analytically strong internal candidate who is not involved with the project. Although the checklists and accompanying guidance provide for more effective controls in the project development process, it is always helpful to have an independent party review the quality of the financial assumptions. This activity is a somewhat easy step that will remove any doubts as to why the project should get approved. (A template is included on page 140 of Chapter 6.) I am confident that any CEO, COO or CFO would fully embrace this idea.

Once you have gained the signatures from all of the required approvers you are ready to get on with the challenging part of the project—the implementation phase. Before beginning though, be sure to communicate the successful results of your business case to the project team. This would also be a good time to pass on to the team any feedback you have gained from the approvers. Acknowledge the support of the team and then take some time to celebrate before the real work begins.

❖

# SOME FINAL THOUGHTS

*I* f you have religiously adhered to all of the recommendations included in this book I know you have experienced a challenging journey preparing your business case. Hopefully you have come to realize that the process is of high value, even if it is very demanding. The rigorous requests for documentation will most likely surprise those companies that have become comfortable with the weak and poorly managed processes they already have in place. When you think of the vast sums of money planned and approved, one would think that improving capital budgeting and business case preparation would be a higher priority for senior management. After all, the future of the company is directly dependent upon the successful outcome of these efforts. As was said before, the preparation of the project business case represents a pivotal transition point for the company, for this is when the long-term strategy is translated into the tactical operating plans used to run the business. How well the strategic objective envisioned by the project is achieved is largely determined by the thoroughness of the project's up-front planning efforts. Can you afford both competitively and financially not to have a sound capital evaluation process?

## WHERE WE HAVE BEEN

As we draw to a close, it is always helpful to step back and review the vast amount of information on capital project analysis that was presented. We began this book by examining the reasons for preparing more detailed business cases and reviewed the problems typically encountered by many companies. Much like corporate mission statements, many will agree that most companies' capital spending policies are largely ceremonial in nature and minimally influence the organization. The directives look good on paper, the executives all say the right words, but no one has demonstrated how those words turn into actions that lead to results.

Desiring to be more action oriented, we systematically reviewed the components of a complete business case and explained why each section was important. Our attention first focused on the business reasoning behind a project. All too often this section is omitted in business cases, and management is left to wonder how the proposal fits into the company's strategy. We also spent considerable energy showing how to prepare a thorough and sound financial analysis. The financial analysis is clearly one of the most important parts of the case in management's eyes. If the project does not make any money, why do it? The financial analysis chapter was designed to help you ask the right questions and to offer advice especially in those circumstances where unprofitable projects must still be done. A more practical approach to sensitivity analysis was also presented in the *'What Can Go Wrong?'* section.

Woven throughout the book's chapters was also advice on how to best "package" your information in a format that management will like and readily approve. The various templates and suggestions provided in this book should come as a great relief for those individuals who are "volunteered" to prepare the business case. No longer will you have to worry about management's expectations when a structured format is followed. For once, you can focus on the substance of the business case and not on its form. Appendix 1—Business Case Templates provides a complete view of all the templates in their proper order of presentation. Cross-references to the appropriate chapters are also included for ease of use in case you need re-read the material. In addition to the templates, a handy glossary of the terminology of project analysis is included in Appendix 2 should you forget a term or just need to enlighten one of the team members.

As you may know, having a well-analyzed and packaged business case does not automatically guarantee success. Getting the right people on the project team is critical. Since projects typically involve people throughout the company, we discussed the steps one should follow to identify and gain agreement on the cross-organizational resources that are often required to implement a project. This kind of advice falls into the well known 'pay me now or pay later' category because it produces benefits (smoother implementation phase) that are primarily downstream of business case preparation. We finished our discussion of business case development by providing guidance on project management and also offered some important tips on how to successfully steer your project through the approval process. I definitely want to acknowledge that a considerable level of effort is required to complete this material. But given the amount of money involved and the strategic nature of capital projects, I think that most senior managers will agree that this level of due diligence on business case preparation is entirely warranted.

**12**

## LESSONS LEARNED

Are there any overriding themes or lessons learned that one should take away after reading this book? The primary lessons all centered on the principles of practicality featured in Chapter 2, with the most important one being communication. Communication is key. Whether it is developing assumptions or getting buy-in from impacted areas and approvers, you must have an effective communication strategy so everyone stays informed. Closely related to this point is recognizing the need to document your work. In today's workplace where assignments are expanding and available resources to work on them are not, it is critical that you take a more formal approach to documenting discussions and agreements among the key project participants. Project managers whose projects are better documented usually find their requests for assistance from impacted areas given higher priority. Written communication is always a powerful tool to hold people accountable for the promises they make.

Another important lesson is to not over-engineer your business case. Being overly precise only adds complexity. Although the contents of the business case seem lengthy, its structure is relatively simple and straightforward. Each section asks only the basic questions that management will want to know. The format is also designed to present a thorough, yet concise, picture of the project to management. And the finished product will be an invaluable asset to the project team. Every member of the team should read the case so they fully understand the business and financial objectives agreed to with management. Individuals who are not informed become liabilities to the team.

> When climbing a mountain, the team can only ascend as fast as the slowest member can climb. Be sure you have selected the best "climbers" for your team and that they are properly prepared before starting the journey.

A final lesson learned involved the assumptions that make up the business case. All too often a lack of discipline in this area leads to the derivation of weak and overly optimistic financial projections. Our discussion emphasized the need to include only those assumptions that are quantifiable and verifiable. Many examples were given that stressed the importance of using quantifiable assumptions that reflect only realistic changes in the company's incremental cash flows. And verifiability focused on the need to measure the results of those assumptions. There is an appropriate saying in business that anyone involved with cost cutting programs will recognize, "If it can't be measured, it can't be saved." Developing assumptions that are both quantifiable and verifiable is the key to producing a high-quality business case that will get your project off to a good start.

The projects your company approves today truly represent the foundation of tomorrow's business. Management should take a more aggressive position on capital project evaluation and recognize that the overall capital spending process is a strategic weapon for the company. Having a disciplined and effective process should be standard practice and not just a nice-to-have procedure or policy. Make sure this strategic weapon is pointed at your competitors and not at yourself.

## Action Items

This would not be a good business book if you did not get a follow-on assignment. If you have taken the time to read this material one can only presume that you are less than thrilled with your company's program to manage capital spending. Now is the time to evaluate the effectiveness of your company's process in order to determine if it is adding value and meeting management's needs. Are the business cases of high quality, and are you seeing results? Are there adequate controls in place?

Capital project evaluation is an area that begs to be standardized and formalized so take the necessary steps to get the process under control in your company. Strive to simplify it, and give people the predictable direction they need. Employees should focus their creative energy on solving problems or creating opportunities that add value to the company and not on struggling with poorly defined processes. Help to unleash the creative genius of your workforce by getting them to focus on the project itself and not on the paperwork. You will see that your employees will welcome the guidance.

> "Predictability is every bit as valuable to employees as it is to customers."
>
> GORDON BETHUNE
> CEO, CONTINENTAL AIRLINES INC.

As you develop a new approach for your company do not forget to plan for sufficient training. It is common to see a good program fail to take root because people were not adequately trained. Depending on the size of your company, give yourself at least twelve months to roll out the new process. This should allow sufficient time to train all project management and other key project personnel. Take personal responsibility for improving your program, and begin today. Your competitors have already started.

## Hold the Vision and Make It So

If you want to do things better, you have to do things different. Holding more meetings and issuing strong management directives to get better or else only dances around the edges of real process improvement. These actions will not lead to the sustainable improvements that are required to turn your weak and ineffective process into a competitive weapon. If you know that your process is not effective, take action now to fix it and then roll the new program out to the organization. Before you start the redesign effort, however, it is imperative that you get the support of the senior management team. You will also have to get the senior players of the operating areas involved as well. Their commitment is essential to ensure compliance from their project managers. Although you would think that support for improving the process would be overwhelming, in reality gaining support never goes as smoothly as one would like. The responses you will receive as you meet with these individuals are fairly predictable and can generally be classified into three groups:

1. **The strong supporters:** are the individuals who create the vision and champion the cause or are strongly aligned with it and actively promote its implementation. This group usually consists of senior managers and the lower-level workers who normally do most of the work. In fact, the lower-level workers may be the most vocal group advocating change.

2. **The fence sitters:** are the individuals who will wait to see if the new ideas will take root before they cast their vote. They are similar to the fair-weather friend who only comes around during good times. These people will jump on board only when it becomes clear that the majority is already in favor of

change. You may get them to agree with your vision, but it is difficult to truly get their commitment. This group usually consists of the mid-level managers and more marginal performers.

3. **The dissidents:** are the individuals who will never be happy with change. These are the company cynics who look to plant rumors with the hopes of undermining or delaying change. These individuals are usually few in number and generally scattered throughout the organization.

Do not let the dissidents stop you from improving the process. Acknowledge that these people exist, and target your improvement campaign on the strong supporters and the fence sitters. Try not to get discouraged if it takes longer than you would like to implement a new process. There will always be stragglers who refuse to change. Hold the vision of a better process, and make it so.

## WHEN YOU NEED HELP

Trying to change a process that has been existence for some time involves changing the company culture, and most of us know that changing the culture is extremely difficult. Many companies resort to bringing in consultants to serve as the change agent. These external parties are usually impartial and provide a good, anonymous sounding board for employees to deliver often-critical commentary to senior management. Since capital budgeting is not a well-centralized function in most companies, you may be faced with a lack of internal resources that can establish new programs and train employees. The Stonehaven Group can assist you with implementing this new vision. We are available to consult with your company regarding implementing any or all or the recommendations presented in this book. Our services include:

- ✧ Providing informational seminars on business case development
- ✧ Developing detailed training sessions for project employees
- ✧ Improving the financial reporting process
- ✧ Customizing materials for your specific needs—including customizing any or all parts of this book!

When you need assistance, contact us:

**www.maximumreturn.net**

The Stonehaven Group
P.O. Box 2455
Walnut Creek, CA 94595
(925) 256-0335

Contact information can always change. Check our website for the most current information. We can help you to build a best-in-class process that will truly add shareholder value now and in the future.

## A WORD ABOUT THE WORKBOOK

This book is designed to serve as an excellent source of information on how to build a better capital evaluation process. I hope it will quickly become a key reference document in every manager's business toolkit. Because of its size, however, it may be too cumbersome to work with on a day-to-day basis. A workbook and booklet series are available that translates the theory in this book into a form more usable for operations personnel.

The *Business Case Planning Workbook* includes:

⟡ High-level chapter summaries to remind you of key points

⟡ Examples of completed business cases to provide guidance on what is acceptable and what is not

⟡ Templates and checklists that you can readily apply to project business cases

The *Maximum Return Series* includes several highly-focused booklets (generally 24 pages in length) designed specifically for the real-time needs of operating groups throughout the organization:

1. **A Capital Project Guide for Project Managers** – 25 Essential Things to Know About Preparing a Business Case

2. **A Capital Project Guide for Senior Managers** – 25 Key Questions to Ask Before You Approve Any Project

3. **A Capital Project Guide for Financial Analysts** – 25 Must-Read Tips on How to "Crunch the Numbers"

4. **Maximum Return Cost Calculator** – Helpful Checklists to Ensure Better Cost Assumptions

5. **Maximum Return Benefit Builder** – Helpful Checklists to Ensure Better Benefit Assumptions

6. **A Capital Project Guide for Auditors** – 25 Key Questions to Ask When Evaluating the Capital Project Process

12

Once people are familiar with the guidance offered in this book, they can turn to the workbook and booklets and use them on the capital project business cases they are preparing. Together this material will meet all of your company's strategic and operational needs surrounding business case development.

Building business cases is an activity that's not just limited to the project developers or analysts in the company. Another book titled *Building Business Cases that Sell Your Products* is also available to give your company a competitive edge in selling its products and services. Just as companies require business cases to purchase things for major projects, this book recognizes the importance of creating a "modified" business case that sales people can offer their prospective clients in order to expedite their buying process. Visit www.maximumreturn.net for information on how to order this or any of the other titles mentioned above.

With this book, you now have a tool that can empower project managers and reviewers to improve perhaps one of the most critical and overlooked processes within the company. The guidance that is offered is theoretically sound, practical and put into terms that employees can readily understand and implement. This is perhaps the one thing that differentiates this book from all others. This book doesn't just espouse theory that has never been field-tested. The recommendations come from many years of direct operational experience. I am confident that you will find your employees grateful and eager to receive consistent direction on how to prepare business cases.

Do not become complacent if your company is just getting by with its present process. You now know better. There can be no turning back once you have stepped through the doorway of greater awareness and have seen a better way. It is now up to you to act. Make it so.

❖

## APPENDIX 1

# BUSINESS CASE TEMPLATES – THE COMPLETE PACKAGE

Appendix

The following templates are taken from Chapters 4 through 10 of this book and are put in the order they would be presented in a business case. They are all combined in this appendix for ease of use. Each template also references the chapter in the book you can turn to for additional information if necessary.

*[Refer to Chapter 4 for additional information on this template]*

# (Your Project Name Here)
# BUSINESS CASE

*Prepared by:*
*Organization:*

*Date:*

*[Refer to Chapter 4 for additional information on this template]*

# TABLE OF CONTENTS

*Substitute the appropriate page number for the **X** that is shown above. For example, if the Executive Summary has four pages, they should be marked: **1.1, 1.2 … 1.4***

*[Refer to Chapter 4 for additional information on this template]*

# EXECUTIVE SUMMARY  Business Case Part 1.x

## PROJECT INFORMATION
Project Name:
Project Sponsor:
Project Manager:

## CATEGORIZATION
❑ New Business      ❑ General/Administrative
❑ Ongoing Support      ❑ Government Required
❑ Other: _____

## RECOMMENDATION
*Briefly state what it is you want to do. What do you want senior management to approve?*

## PROJECT DESCRIPTION
*Briefly describe the project including its objective and the nature of the costs and benefits.*

[Be mindful that the section numbers in the upper right corners of the business case templates do not correspond to the number of the chapters they are reviewed in. For instance, Business Case section 1 is reviewed in Chapter 4; section 2 is in Chapter 5, and so on.]

*[Refer to Chapter 4 for additional information on this template]*

# EXECUTIVE SUMMARY    *Business Case Part1.x*

## FINANCIAL SUMMARY

|  | Present Year | Year 1 | Year 2 | Year 3... (through the life of the project) |
|---|---|---|---|---|
| Net Income | $ | | | |
| Cash Flow | $ | | | |

Capital Investment:
NPV @ ___% Discount Rate:
IRR:
Payback:
Capital Investment Included in Budget? ❑ Yes  ❑ No  ❑ Partially

*You will tailor this section to the financial methods that you will be using for evaluating your project. The financial methods are reviewed in Chapter 6. Always keep the information at a very high level.*

## ABBREVIATED TIMETABLE

Start Date:
Major Milestone Dates:
Finish Date:

*Include the starting and ending dates of the project at a minimum. You may also include the dates of any significant milestones if known.*

*[Refer to Chapter 4 for additional information on this template]*

## EXECUTIVE SUMMARY                    *1.x*

### APPROVAL SECTION

Project Authorization

_____    _____
Name & Title                                    Date

_____    _____
Name & Title                                    Date

_____    _____
Name & Title                                    Date

_____    _____
Name & Title                                    Date

### IMPACTED AREA APPROVAL

_____    _____
Name & Title & Organization                Date

_____    _____
Name & Title & Organization                Date

_____    _____
Name & Title & Organization                Date

*Include signature blocks for the normal approval hierarchy in your company. Also provide an approval section for the managers of any key areas impacted by the project.*

*[Refer to Chapter 5 for additional information on this template]*

## BUSINESS ANALYSIS          *Business Case Part 2.x*

### STATEMENT OF THE PROBLEM/ISSUE/OPPORTUNITY
*Provide a concise statement of the problem, issue or opportunity the project is trying to resolve or act upon.*

### DISCUSSION OF HISTORICAL CONTEXT
*Include any prior history of the project here, especially if the project experienced difficulties in the past.*

### DISCUSSION OF ALTERNATIVES CONSIDERED

Lower-Cost Alternative: *Are there ways to address the problem if you were only given half the money?*

Higher-Cost Alternative: *What ways could you address the problem if money is no object?*

Do-Nothing Alternative: *What is the impact of delaying the project one year?*

### FIT WITH COMPANY GOALS & STRATEGY
*How does the project fit with goals and strategy of the company?*

*[Refer to Chapter 6 for additional information on this template]*

# FINANCIAL ANALYSIS  *Business Case Part 3.x*

## INCOME STATEMENT AND CASH FLOWS

| | Year 0 | Year 1 | Year 2... |
|---|---|---|---|
| INCOME STATEMENT | | | (through the life of the project) |

Project Benefits
  Added Revenues
  Cost Reductions

**Total Benefits**

Project Costs
  Implementation
  Other…

**Total Costs**

Depreciation of Investment

**Profit Before Taxes**

Taxes @ ____%

**Profit After Taxes**

CASH FLOW ADJUSTMENTS
Capital Investment
ImplementationCosts
  (Capitalized)
Add Back Non-Cash Items

**Cash Flow**

## EVALUATION OF CASH FLOWS

| | Project Results | Company Requirement |
|---|---|---|
| IRR | ____% | ____% |
| NPV(Discounted at ___%) | $_____ | $_____ |
| Payback | Between year ____ and year ____ | Between year____ and year____ |

*[Refer to Chapter 6 for additional information on this template]*

# FINANCIAL ANALYSIS                                      3.x

## COST SUMMARY

| | Initial Investment | Year 1 | Year 2... (through the life of the project) |
|---|---|---|---|
| Cost Item A | | | |
| Cost Item B | | | |
| Cost Item C | | | |
| Total Capital Investment Costs | | | |
| | | | |
| Cost Item D | | | |
| Cost Item E | | | |
| Cost Item F | | | |
| Cost Item G | | | |
| Cost Item H | | | |
| Total Implementation Costs | | | |
| | | | |
| Depreciation | | | |
| | | | |
| Other | | | |
| | | | |
| Total Costs | | | |

*Provide a summary of your project cost assumptions. It will help to categorize your costs where possible as is shown in this example.*

*[Refer to Chapter 6 for additional information on this template]*

# FINANCIAL ANALYSIS   *Business Case Part 3.x*

## BENEFIT SUMMARY

| | Year 1 | Year 2... (through the life of the project) |
|---|---|---|
| Benefit Item A | | |
| Benefit Item B | | |
| Benefit Item C | | |
|    Total Added Revenues | | |
| | | |
| Benefit Item D | | |
| Benefit Item E | | |
| Benefit Item F | | |
| Benefit Item G | | |
| Benefit Item H | | |
|    Total Cost Reductions | | |
| | | |
|    Total Benefits | | |

*Provide a summary of your project benefit assumptions. It will help to categorize your benefits where possible as is shown in this example. Complete the benefit checklists on pages 110-112 for each item, and include them in the appendix.*

*[Refer to Chapter 6 for additional information on this template]*

## FINANCIAL ANALYSIS  *Business Case Part 3.x*

### IMPACT TO BUDGET

|  | Business Case | Project Dollars Included In<br>Approved Budget | Variance |
|---|---|---|---|
| Capital | $ | | |
| Benefits | $ | | |
| Expense | $ | | |

Explanation of Variance

Capital:

Benefits:

Expense:

*List the reasons for each variance. If only part of the project is budgeted, explain why. If none of the project is budgeted, explain why it was not included. Also include a discussion of how any negative variances will be overcome.*

*[Refer to Chapter 6 for additional information on this template]*

# FINANCIAL ANALYSIS  *Business Case Part 3.x*

## FINANCIAL ATTESTATION

❑  Financial analysis acceptable; estimates are conservative
❑  Financial analysis acceptable; estimates are not conservative
❑  Financial analysis marginal; exceptions are noted below
❑  Other (Explain)

Exceptions
Item                                    Responsible Individual

Signature

_____          _____

Financial Analyst Reviewing the Case      Date
Analyst's Business Area

*Assign a financial analyst not directly connected with the project to review the financial analysis including the assumptions behind the cost and benefit analysis. Note any exceptions and have the analyst sign and date the form.*

*[Refer to Chapter 7 for additional information on this template]*

# WHAT CAN GO WRONG?  *Business Case Part 4.x*

## TOP-FIVE CRITICAL DRIVERS
*What are the top-five mission critical drivers for this project? (The project would not succeed if these five things were not done right.)*

## SENSITIVITY ANALYSIS
Include a brief discussion of the potential risk to the project in the following areas:

Economic Risk

Schedule Risk

Market Risk

Technology Risk

Government/Regulatory Risk

Other

*Modify these categories to suit your particular business situation. Include any assumption checklists in the appendix.*

*[Refer to Chapter 8 for additional information on this template]*

# IMPACT ANALYSIS  *Business Case Part 5.x*

## IMPACT ON OTHER DEPARTMENTS
*Discuss what departments are affected by or are needed to support the project. Also discuss **how** these departments are impacted.*

## IMPACT ON OTHER PROJECTS
*Discuss if this project impacts any other projects that may be ongoing in the company.*

## IMPACT ON EXTERNAL GROUPS
*Discuss if there is an impact to any groups outside the company.*

*[Refer to Chapter 9 for additional information on this template]*

# PROJECT MANAGEMENT   *Business Case Part 6.x*

## APPROVAL HIERARCHY

*Provide an organizational view of the project approval hierarchy. Also include any areas impacted by the project.*

## PROJECT TEAM

*Provide an organizational view of the project team.*

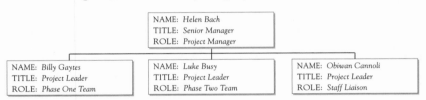

## PROJECT MANAGER

*Include a brief description of the project manager's qualifications.*

## TEAM MEMBER QUALIFICATIONS

*Include a brief description of the qualifications of each of the team members if they are known at the time the proposal is prepared. If you do not know the team members, you may wish to discuss the qualifications of the roles you desire to fill.*

*[Refer to Chapter 9 for additional information on this template]*

## PROJECT MANAGEMENT *Business Case Part 6.x*

### TIMETABLE

*Develop a high-level timetable that can convey significant tasks that are anticipated in the project. Include a separate line for each major activity or milestone of the project (if they are known).*

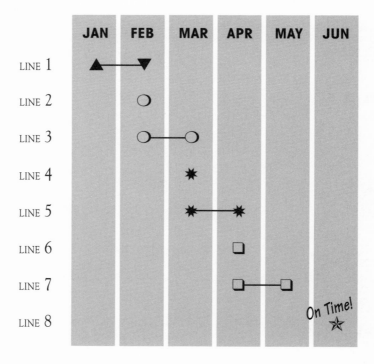

*[Refer to Chapter 10 for additional information on this template]*

# APPENDIX
## Business Case Part 7.x

**Item:**          *State the item being reviewed*
                   (e.g. Tax rate calculation)

**Definition:**    *Describe the item; give the formula if necessary*
                   (e.g. ROI = Average Profit After Taxes/Average
                    Project Investment)

**Results:**       *Show the result of the calculation*
                   (e.g. IRR = 25%)

## Additional Information:

*Show the actual calculation of the result if a complex formula is used.*
*Remove any source of doubt as to how the numbers are generated.*

(e.g. WACC  = (After Tax Cost of Debt * Percentage of Debt Used)

       + (Cost of Preferred Stock * Percentage of Preferred Used)

       + (Cost of Equity * Percentage of Equity Used)

       = (10% * 30%) + (12% * 10%) + (15% * 60%)

       = 13.2% )

## Areas Consulted:

*List the key contacts you consulted in preparing the assumption or analysis.*
(e.g. Seymour Monee, Assistant Treasurer consulted on the
 derivation of the cost of capital)

# THE LANGUAGE OF PROJECT ANALYSIS

**Benefits** – Benefits are the primary reason a project is undertaken. They typically fall into two categories—added revenues and cost reductions. A benefit assumption is considered "good" when someone can easily visualize the assumption being turned into cash once the project is fully implemented.

**Bean Counter** – An endearing term that operating people frequently call financial analysts who work on business cases.

**Budget Process** – The activities that occur during the period of time when a company establishes its next fiscal year's operating targets. The focus may be on setting operational goals and/or levels of capital spending. Companies often refer to the process of establishing capital targets as the "capital budgeting process."

**Business Case** – The formal document that is prepared for justifying a project's value. The goal of the business case is to convince management of the project's worthiness and thereby secure funding. A business case is analogous to the loan request an individual prepares when asking for a bank loan.

**Capital** – The money a company invests in a project. The source of the money is often from a combination of equity (retained earnings or new equity), preferred stock or debt. Shareholders will demand an adequate return (one that is commensurate with the risk being assumed) for the money that is lent to do the project.

**Capital Project** – Any project that requires the use of company funds. The more funds that are needed, the tighter the controls a company will usually place on the management of the project.

**Cash Flow** – The actual movement of money into or out of the project. It is not to be confused with how accounting records transactions under the accrual method of accounting. Depreciation is an example of a non-cash flow cost because it represents an accounting concept that seeks to match an asset's costs with the benefits gained over its useful life. Cash flow calculations are used for evaluating the financial worthiness of a project.

**Contingency** – Usually labeled as "management contingency," contingency builds conservatism into the financial analysis by understating profitability. Contingencies can also take the form of understated benefits or overstated cost assumptions.

**Cost of Capital** – Commonly referred to as the "hurdle rate," the Cost of Capital is the rate of return a project must clear (i.e. the project must earn a greater rate of return) in order for it to add shareholder value.

**Costs** – Project costs represent the outflows of real cash that typically occur early in the project's life cycle. These costs should only reflect incremental costs; that is, the cost would go away if the project ceased to exist.

**Critical Driver** – The things or activities that would have to be done right if the project is to succeed. Failure to focus on the critical drivers could put the project's goals at great risk.

**Depreciation** – An accounting concept for matching the cost of an asset with the revenue earned over the projected lifespan of the asset. Depreciation is included in the calculation of a project's "book" income but is excluded in the calculation of cash flow. Consult with Fixed Asset Accounting to determine the proper depreciation figures for the project assets.

**Impacted Area** – An area outside of the project's sponsoring organization that could be affected in some way by the project. The project may require support from such an area or the project may have an effect on that area's operating performance. The project team must keep all impacted areas fully apprised of the project's objectives and status.

**Internal Rate of Return (IRR)** – IRR is the return one would expect to earn on a project's capital investment. Specifically, the value of IRR represents the rate at which the present value of the project's investment costs exactly equals the present value of its benefits. It is one of the most widely used measures for evaluating projects, and it should always be compared to the cost of capital. If the IRR is greater, then shareholder value is created.

Appendix

**Net Present Value (NPV)** – NPV is the preferred method for evaluating projects because it takes into account the time value of money and the cost of money used to fund the project. It is calculated by discounting the project's cash flows by the cost of capital. NPVs greater than zero add shareholder value.

**Payback** – The length of time it takes for a project to break even on its initial investment. A derivative calculation called "discounted payback" discounts the project's benefits at the company's cost of capital. Payback can be very misleading if used by itself.

**Propeller Head** – An endearing term that financial analysts frequently call technology people who are oblivious to finance.

**Return on Investment (ROI)** – ROI measures how much is earned on the company's capital that is invested in the project.

**Sensitivity Analysis** – An analysis of key operating variables affecting the project. It tries to determine how much volatility is in the data by examining various critical drivers such as economic, technology or market conditions. Sensitivity analysis frequently requires the analyst to ask, "What can go wrong with the assumption under review?"

**Sunk Costs** – Costs that are associated with past activities and are not relevant to a project's analysis. If you think the action was related to the project but the money was already spent, it is a sunk cost and should be ignored.

**Timeline** – The timeline for the analysis should generally be equal to the expected life of the project. (e.g. technology projects typically have very short timelines.) Consult with your fixed asset accountant to determine the proper timeline.

## APPENDIX 3

# WHY PROJECT APPROVAL IS SO CHALLENGING

Appendix

I f developing business cases is so important, why haven't most companies figured out a better way to manage this process? Why all the confusion and frustration around this topic? Let's face it—analyzing capital projects and getting them approved is a difficult and complex task. Perhaps the one thing making it so difficult is the "score keeping."

The accounting treatment for capital is very confusing to many managers, and often there is a limited understanding of how capital spending decisions impact the company's financial statements. Because bonuses are typically tied to "bottom-line" performance, there is usually little incentive for managers to worry about capital programs where the financial impact is spread over many years. Our business culture is more interested in immediate results. It doesn't mean that you should ignore capital spending. It just points out that people will tend to spend more energy on those things that impact short-term financial results because that is how they are compensated. Hence, more effort is focused on controlling expense budgets and increasing revenues than on managing capital spending. Even though Wall Street analysts say they always look at the long-term viability of a company, look at Wall Street's reaction to a company's stock price if its earnings fail to meet analyst's expectations. Sometimes it seems as if nobody is focused on the long term.

The complexity involved in financial modeling is also beyond many managers' comprehension (or interest) which often yields a "don't-bother-me-with-the-details" attitude. I am reminded of a manager who, during program reviews would dose off if the material got too detailed. Not only was this rude, but I was always concerned that he would injure himself if he were ever to fall from his chair. Complexity is also a highly subjective term. What may be complex for some (and perhaps physically threatening if you risk falling out of chairs) may be light reading for another. Generally speaking, complexities in the evaluation process include determining how to properly analyze the project on financial terms. Seemingly simple questions have few straightforward answers:

✧ How are the benefits determined?

✧ How do we treat items such as productivity improvements, avoided costs or other intangibles?

✧ Should we use IRR, NPV, payback or something else?

✧ What exactly are IRR and NPV? Is one better than the other?

✧ Who decides on the hurdle rate, and what is a hurdle rate?

✧ How do I know if I have the right cash flows in my analysis? How do I calculate cash flow?

The term cash flow that is mentioned in the last question is another area that is confusing to most people. As mentioned before, most of the people involved with project approval do not understand the complexities of accounting. What financial information they do see is usually developed using an accrual basis of accounting, not a cash basis. [At a **very** high level—cash accounting only records activity when actual cash changes hands, such as you paying a bill or receiving revenue. You run your house on a cash basis. An accrual basis accounts for the promises that people make during the course of business, such as I promise to pay your company for these goods in 30 days. A company will "book" the sale although it hasn't received any money yet.] Although on the surface this does not seem like a big deal, educating people on the finer points of cash flow analysis and how it reconciles to their monthly financial statements is quite difficult.

Finally, many project development efforts cross organizational lines thereby confusing matters greatly. While it may be clear who is ultimately responsible for the project (i.e. where the buck stops), a lot of finger pointing may be going on behind the scenes if the project is not aggressively managed. As many know from experience, poor communication is one of the biggest obstacles to successful project implementation. The process as outlined in this book helps to address many of these concerns.

Most people who work on projects would rather focus on the fun part—the project itself. Nobody wants to deal with the paperwork or especially the financial theory. Although we can appreciate that feeling, it is still our fiduciary responsibility as managers to provide a thorough and quality evaluation of every project. Doing the appropriate analysis and properly packaging the material for review becomes a very critical step in a project's life cycle.

Despite all the challenges mentioned above, it is hard to provide a convincing argument that companies should not actively manage their capital resources. And despite all the complexities, project managers and sponsors must be held accountable for providing an adequate return to the owners of the company. Only by providing practical guidance on business case development can we improve the odds of success in this important area.

Appendix

It is quite surprising how very little is standardized when it comes to analyzing projects and preparing business cases. Certainly much has been written about the finance-side of project analysis—it is a topic that is included in every undergraduate and graduate-level college finance curriculum. But very little is written on the practical side that answers such questions as:

How much analysis is required?

What do you do once your financial analysis is completed?

How do you package your work and "sell" it to management?

How do you get the organization to support your project?

The only guidance traditionally available to companies has been the academic finance theory one usually finds in textbooks. Usually these resources are seldom helpful because they go into so much complexity and professorial theories that most management teams get lost in the detail.

APPENDIX 4

# BUSINESS CASE DEVELOPMENT – THE MYTH & THE REALITY

Appendix

C apital project evaluation or capital budgeting is usually a process most people are unwilling to discuss in much detail. Many are hesitant to admit to the effectiveness or ineffectiveness of their efforts. Capital spending budgets in some companies are quite large and to confess to not having a well-controlled process could be career limiting. As you attend seminars or talk to others on this subject, it is easy to become discouraged. Everyone will tell you about the wonderful job their company is doing in managing capital projects. However, the truth is many companies do a poor job.

In *Why Project Approval is so Challenging* (see Appendix 3), I discussed some of the underlying reasons why capital budgeting has become such a "second-class" activity. In *Business Case Development – The Myth & The Reality* I share some of my experiences to let you know that you're not alone if your company's process is in need of repair. I also talk briefly about companies that do manage this process well and if there are any lessons learned that one can take away.

## THE MYTH – "OUR CAPITAL PROCESS IS WELL MANAGED"

At a finance seminar attended by managers of many capital-intensive companies, I had an opportunity to inquire into the processes used by their companies to manage business case development. At first, listening to their stories made me feel quite envious. The typical response given by finance managers to my inquiry was: "Oh, our process is very good. Our people developed it themselves!" Wishing to be enlightened by my peers, I probed a little deeper and discovered that the "very good" process turned out to be nothing more than a financial analyst's spreadsheet program. It turns out that most of the companies I talked to manage this important process by hand with often little or no formal guidance given to the field.

## THE REALITY

Does anybody do a good job evaluating capital projects? One would certainly expect that capital-intensive companies would have a head start down the path of greater understanding. Automobile companies, utilities, oil and gas companies and high-technology companies are examples of industries where capital requirements are high. You might think that because of the shear size of some of these businesses, the issue of managing project evaluations would already be figured out. As many people will attest to, however, bigger does not necessarily mean better. For many, bigger usually implies more bureaucracy which in turn means any process will be more difficult to manage.

Some capital-intensive companies, such as those with heavy research and development requirements, have made great strides toward developing sophisticated capital evaluation processes. The pharmaceutical industry is an excellent example of an industry with great needs for effective project management. This industry offers unique challenges unlike many others. Tremendous amounts of money are funneled into developmental drug programs where scientific uncertainty and governmental regulation conspire to make successful outcomes highly uncertain. Finding out if a project is successful can often take many years. It is very easy for a company to take up to ten years, spending hundreds of millions of dollars, to bring a drug to market. And even when a drug makes it to the market, there is no guarantee that it will return the cost of the capital the company has invested in its development. Because of this high stakes environment, many pharmaceutical companies are very aggressive in managing their financial resources. These companies are often very quantitative and analytically focused. Many have developed in-house computer programs that include the use of sophisticated concepts like Monte Carlo simulation and option theory to evaluate the projects they manage. In order to take advantage of these techniques, however, a company must possess an extensive historical database of information on the effectiveness of its project programs.

The sophisticated and scientific approach to financial management taken by many pharmaceutical firms sets them apart from most other companies. In reality, most companies will probably find the cultural hurdle (of using a highly scientific approach to finance) and the associated costs just too great to manage. While it is true that the concepts used in the pharmaceutical industry would be extremely helpful to any business, many companies cannot afford the extensive system requirements and the high-priced talent needed to operate them. Even if you could afford it, educating management on the finer points of Monte Carlo simulation and option theory may be too daunting a task. Managing capital spending, although still very important, is not as consuming a priority for many companies as it is in the pharmaceutical industry.

Most company approaches to capital project evaluation are usually home grown or ad-hoc in nature—most likely starting off as a process developed on some analyst's personal computer. Companies with bigger finance departments usually have the talent to design their own computer programs, customizing them to their unique requirements. The problem with many of these homegrown methods is that they focus solely on financial evaluation. Little to no effort is placed on examining the business issues underlying the financial assumptions. Little to no effort is ever spent ensuring that the project's goals and requirements are properly communicated throughout the organization. And little to no effort is ever focused on developing adequate briefings to senior management. These additional (and often overlooked) steps are the actions that will improve the odds of success for the project.

Chances are that if you have requirements similar to those described in the pharmaceutical industry, you are probably in big trouble if you're reading this book. That industry, and others like it (e.g. biotechnology), requires very sophisticated methods for managing capital projects that are out of the scope of this book. The advice offered in *Maximum Return* is aimed at those companies that don't demand such sophistication but nevertheless still desire a highly disciplined and well-controlled capital spending process.

## APPENDIX 5

# OTHER COST ASSUMPTION GUIDANCE

Appendix

The following information reviews several subject areas that typically confuse people during the preparation of the cost assumptions. Review each part closely to see if it applies to your project.

## PROBABILITY

As your fill out the checklists, you may have developed a range of probable outcomes for your assumptions. Some companies, such as those with large research and development requirements, tend to be more analytical and are quite skilled at determining probability distributions for their cost assumptions. In these cases it is important to use the expected value of the cost assumption as calculated by the weighted-average of the different probable outcomes.

## EXAMPLE

Calculating the Probable Outcome for a Cost Assumption:

| Financial Estimate | | Probability of Occurrence | |
|---|---|---|---|
| $2,000 | * | 50% | |
| $2,500 | * | 30% | $2,350 Cost Estimate |
| $3,000 | * | 20% | |

If you are like most companies, it is hard enough to determine one probable outcome yet alone two or more. If your company has more sophisticated analytical needs and capabilities, insert them into the checklist. The checklist is easily adaptable to any analytical situation.

## INFLATION

Another item included in the checklist is inflation. You generally have two choices when preparing cost estimates: include the effects of inflation or not include them. Inflation is a fact of life in most countries and must be considered in the financial analysis of your project. Most companies tend to include the effects of inflation, but this is often a difficult process that involves determining the correct escalators to apply for the project's different types of costs. For example, labor is escalated differently than computers or materials. Usually the individuals responsible for managing or purchasing those items in your company can help you determine the proper inflation factors to incorporate in your analysis. Your company may even have an economics function that monitors such information. Consult your controller or finance representative for guidance on good sources of inflation escalators.

Whether you choose to include inflation or not, it is important that your cost estimates are consistent with the way the cost of capital is calculated. (The cost of capital is reviewed in Appendix 8.) The cost of capital, as typically determined by most companies, includes a premium for inflation. You must apply consistent inflation assumptions in your analysis in order to evaluate accurately your project's financial value. For example, if your cash flows exclude inflation and your cost of capital includes inflation, a common error, then the resultant *net present value* for your project will be biased downward. In other words, the results are worse than they should be if the analysis was done correctly.

Inflation is an extremely important item to consider when preparing the financial analysis of your project. Because you are dealing with the future, one must accept that estimating inflation adds yet another degree of uncertainty into an already complex process. Understanding the basis of your inflation assumptions and thoroughly documenting them will help you build a sound financial projection.

## SUNK COSTS

Another cost topic that is familiar to most people, but bears repeating anyway, is sunk costs. Sunk costs are costs that are associated with past activities. Although those activities may be related to your project, they are no longer relevant to your present analysis since they occurred in the past. You cannot undo any of those prior actions because the money was already spent. Most people in business are quite aware of the concept of sunk costs and know never to include them in project analysis. Even with this knowledge, I am still amazed at the poor business decisions that people make because of sunk costs as is shown in the following example.

Appendix

At one company, a $30 million software development project for its sales force was running into trouble. After having spent half of its money, the project was woefully behind schedule, and there was nothing to show for its investment. No tangible progress was made in designing the sales tool the company desperately needed if it was to stay competitive. Although, the project team seemed hopelessly lost, they still pleaded for more money to "complete the vision." They proposed a new plan that shared some similarity with the original plan—it shared the same name. Everything else about the project was different. The change in project scope signaled the perfect time to redo the business case, however, project management was opposed to updating it. Instead, they insisted that the project's new direction fully intended to "live up to the spirit" of the original business case. The real story was that no one wanted to confess to management that they had nothing to show for spending $15 million. There was fear that many project team members would lose their jobs if the truth was discovered. The team had too much invested in the project to stop. They had to deliver something! Several million more dollars were spent before management finally decided to halt the project.

Be leery of sunk costs. Although everyone knows you should never consider sunk costs in future decision making, it is easy to get trapped in the same situation as described above if the stakes are high enough. Like the gambler who has lost a lot of money and is trying to make up for it with one last roll of the dice, all the theory of sunk costs can quickly fly out the window if your project is faced with big losses and your career is potentially on the line.

## OPPORTUNITY COSTS

The topic of opportunity costs is another area that is very familiar to people but often confusing in financial analysis. Opportunity costs are best described by means of an example. Suppose your project involves building a new facility and you are given two alternatives. Alternative 1 is to build the facility on a parcel of land already owned by the company. Alternative 2 is to build the facility in a location that is not owned by the company. Alternative 2 differs from alternative 1 because there is an additional cost of acquiring the land. It is quite obvious that the analysis should include the cost of the land in Alternative 2, but what should you do about the land in Alternative 1? Many people might argue that you should *exclude* the land because the company incurs no additional cost. While this is a tempting argument, the correct choice is to include a cost that approximates the land's market value. The analysis should include the market price for the land because the company can choose to sell the parcel rather than build on it. In this example, you can consult a local real estate professional in order to obtain the market value of the property. Always incorporate opportunity costs in your analysis should similar situations like this arise. It may involve additional work on your part to determine the item's market value, but the resulting analysis is more meaningful.

## FINANCING CHARGES

As you go about building the cash flows for your project's cost assumptions be careful **not** to include an assumption for financing costs. Financing costs represent the interest charges on the money you borrow in order to fund the project. Including these charges in your cash flows will lead to inaccurate results when calculating the project's net present value (NPV) or internal rate of return (IRR). (NPV and IRR are two measures for evaluating the financial worthiness of a project.) You would be effectively double counting the cost of financing the project by discounting your cash flows at your company's weighted-average cost of capital. Most companies finance their capital projects with a mix of debt and equity, and the weighted-average cost of capital accounts for each company's specific mix of financing. The resultant weighted-average rate represents the financing charge assessed to the project. Do not add that cost again as a separate cash flow assumption. Discuss this item with your finance representative if you are uncertain as to whether you are handling this assumption properly.

## OTHER COST ADVICE

As you develop your cost assumptions (and benefits too) you must be aware of your project's potential impact on other activities within the company. It is important for you to account (in your cost and benefit analysis) for any impacts to other programs or projects that may already be underway. If your project does change the financial projections (favorably or unfavorably) for some other activity, then include those changes in your cost estimates.

Lastly, sometimes your project may be large enough to impact the company's net working capital requirements. Net working capital is the name given to the netting of current assets (e.g. cash, accounts receivable, inventories) and current liabilities (e.g. accounts payable, short-term liabilities). If the project involves adding an entire new product line, for example, one would expect that the company's net working capital requirements would have to change. Higher sales would translate into higher accounts receivable and inventories and also higher payables to new suppliers. Include any additions to net working capital in your analysis. You may want to consult with a financial analyst or someone in your controller's office for advice on this matter if you are not sure whether your project impacts the company's net working capital position. If you do include something for net working capital be sure to back it out of your analysis in the last year. Theoretically speaking, the company no longer needs to support the higher level of net working capital once the project is completed. The analysis in the final year should reflect the conditions that existed prior to the project's existence.

## APPENDIX 6

# DEPRECIATION

Almost every capital project requires the purchasing of fixed assets. Although the capital outlay for the asset usually occurs early in the project, the total cost must be depreciated for financial statement purposes over the life of the asset. Depreciation is a key element in the calculation of net income and cash flow, and as you may know from basic accounting courses, there are many different ways to calculate depreciation. Straight line, double declining balance and sum-of-the-years digits are but a few choices. Please consult your accounting department if you are interested in learning more about other depreciation methods and how they are calculated.

As you prepare your financial projections, it is important to use the correct depreciation methodology that applies to the asset you are acquiring. Most companies use different methods of depreciation when determining net income as reported to shareholders (book purposes) and net income as reported for tax purposes. Make it a point to consult with the individual in your company who is responsible for fixed asset accounting. Depreciation is not an assumption to guess on when resources are readily available to provide better guidance. This is especially important because the depreciation schedules used by accounting are not always in line with the true economic lives of the assets purchased. The correct values to use in your analysis are the ones recognized by accounting.

Depreciation is also an important value when it comes time to calculating a project's cash flow. Depreciation is often called a non-cash charge, and its actual value must **not** be included in the final cash flow figures. It is called a non-cash charge because, in any one year, depreciation (as reflected on the book income statements) only represents a portion of the asset's original cost. No cash is ever paid out when these annual entries are made. The actual cash disbursement was made when the asset was purchased.

The complexity of how depreciation is handled in your cash flow analysis depends on whether your company uses different depreciation methods for book and tax purposes. The analysis is very straightforward if the methodologies are the same. If the methodologies are different, buckle your seat belt because the analysis can be confusing. Consult with your accounting staff if you are not sure whether your company uses different depreciation methods for book and tax purposes. The following is a high-level series of steps for incorporating depreciation into your cash flow analysis:

## Are your book and tax methods for depreciation the same?

| SAME | DIFFERENT |
|---|---|
| **Action for Calculating Cash Flow** | **Action for Calculating Cash Flow** |
| 1. Back out pretax depreciation expense. | 1. Back out pretax book depreciation expense. |
| 2. Analysis finished. | 2. Back out **tax effect** of book depreciation expense. (*Tax rate * Depreciation Expense-Book*) |
| | 3. Add back **tax effect** using depreciation used for tax purposes. (*Tax rate * Depreciation Expense-Tax*) |
| | 4. Analysis finished. |

As indicated above, your analysis is very straightforward if you have consistent depreciation methodologies for book and tax purposes. Simply back out the pretax depreciation expense from your book income statements in order to calculate cash flow. The analysis becomes more complex when the methodologies differ. Since the actual cash payment of income taxes is calculated from the tax set of financial statements (or tax books), you must account for the tax effect of depreciation in your cash flow analysis. (Company income taxes are actually reduced because depreciation is tax deductible.) An example will help clarify this issue.

## EXAMPLE

Appendix

| | |
|---|---|
| Asset Cost: | $500 |
| Depreciable Life: | 5 years |
| Book Depreciation Method: | Straight Line |
| Tax Depreciation Method: | Double Declining Balance |
| Tax Rate: | 40% |

**Depreciation for Book Purposes**

| | Year 1 | Year 2 | Year 3 | Year 4 | Year 5 | Exclude/Include from Cash Flow |
|---|---|---|---|---|---|---|
| Depreciation Expense | $ 100 | $ 100 | $ 100 | $ 100 | $ 100 | Exclude |
| Income Taxes Payable | (40) | (40) | (40) | (40) | (40) | Exclude |
| After-tax Expense Books | $ 60 | $ 60 | $ 60 | $ 60 | $ 60 | |

**Depreciation for Tax Purposes**

| | Year 1 | Year 2 | Year 3 | Year 4 | Year 5 | |
|---|---|---|---|---|---|---|
| Depreciation Expense | $ 200 | $ 120 | $ 72 | $ 43 | $ 65 | Ignore |
| Income Taxes Payable | (80) | (48) | (29) | (17) | (26) | Include |
| After-tax Expense Tax Purposes | $ 120 | $ 72 | $ 43 | $ 26 | $ 39 | |

The cash flow analysis for each year should include the tax deductibility of the depreciation expense as calculated by tax accounting. This concept is very confusing and most companies are either unaware of this issue or choose to ignore it because of its complexity. Is the difference in the tax calculation for book and tax purposes really material? It depends. The difference could be material if there are several projects competing for funding. In such cases, greater precision in the analysis is required. It would not be considered material if there are no other competing projects, and the project under review has an acceptable rate of return using the book method. You are effectively building conservatism into your analysis if the depreciation method for tax purposes is more accelerated than the method used for book purposes. Management might find this approach perfectly acceptable.

# APPENDIX 7

# TAXES

After going through all of the work of preparing the cost and benefit assumptions, the last thing most people want to do is spend time on taxes. Paying taxes is one of the facts of life that everyone can relate to on a personal level. You must also consider them as you prepare the net income and cash flow projections for your project. Because shareholders or owners of the business are only interested in the benefits that end up in their pocket, project analysis must always be done on an *after-tax basis*.

There are three areas involving taxes that require review:

- ✧ Special cost assumptions involving taxes
- ✧ The marginal tax rate used to calculate the project's profit after taxes
- ✧ The tax impact of using different depreciation methods (please refer to Appendix 6 for a discussion of this item)

The most overlooked items in developing a project's cost assumptions are sales/use taxes and property taxes associated with the purchase of the project's assets. These taxes vary greatly by geographic area, and it is most important that you review your fixed asset purchases with your tax accountant to ensure that appropriate tax assumptions are included in your analysis. Your tax accountant can also do a more effective job of tax planning for your company if you proactively involve him or her in your business case preparation.

The other area that remains confusing is choosing the tax rate to apply to the project's profit before taxes. The tax rate used for project analysis is called the marginal tax rate and represents the tax rate paid on each additional dollar of income earned by the company. Federal taxes and state or provincial taxes are the two components of the tax rate and they vary greatly from company to company. As you might suspect, tax rates are extremely difficult to predict and are affected by many factors including:

✧ Changes in the tax laws by federal, state or provincial governments,

✧ Future profitability of the company,

✧ Special tax considerations like net operating loss carry forwards, and

✧ Tax impacts associated with any acquisitions or divestitures.

Including specific guidance on tax policy is somewhat problematic because of the volatility of the tax laws. Anything written today becomes quickly outdated tomorrow. Consult with your company's tax accounting department to obtain the tax rate projections for your financial analysis. I strongly recommend that your company's finance group assume the responsibility for working with the tax area to develop a consistent set of assumptions for company-wide use. Doing so would avoid the problem having ten different tax rates for ten different projects. Develop one marginal tax rate assumption for your company and stick with it! To do otherwise would greatly increase the complexity of the analysis and confuse the project teams. Of course, there may be times when taxes are the sole reason for doing a project. It is imperative to strive for greater precision in the tax assumptions in these kinds of cases.

Because of the complexity of tax accounting, many of us employ some other person or company to prepare our personal income tax returns. We should acknowledge that company tax returns are far more complicated and not resort to guessing when developing a project's tax assumptions. Unless your company is not required to file tax returns, we know that there is always someone you can turn to for advice. Now would probably be a good time to take your tax person out to lunch if you have not already done so.

**A P P E N D I X   8**

# COST OF CAPITAL

The calculation of the cost of capital is the closest thing you will find to a "black box" in most companies. In some companies, the cost of capital has not changed for decades even though most have experienced big changes in their business. Most people are not really sure how the number is calculated or who is responsible for providing it. When questioned about the derivation of the cost of capital most analysts simply respond, "But this is what we've always used in the past." Despite the confusion, the cost of capital is probably the most important measure used in capital project evaluation. Unless there are special circumstances, projects are typically not approved if they cannot earn more than their company's cost of capital. This measure helps management gauge whether the project will "show them the money."

The cost of capital is used in project analysis for calculating a project's net present value or NPV. It is commonly called the *discount rate* because it represents the value used to discount the project's future cash flows to present conditions. Also referred to as the *hurdle rate*, the cost of capital is often compared to other evaluation techniques such as the internal rate of return or IRR. The IRR of a project must exceed or "clear" the company's hurdle rate for it to be worthy of consideration.

There are two things to keep in mind when calculating the cost of capital:

1. Costs should reflect the marginal cost of new debt, preferred stock and common equity and not historical costs. (Historical costs are not relevant because these

projects will occur in the future.)

2. Always include the effect of taxes in your calculation. (The interest on debt is a tax-deductible expense and must be factored into the overall cost of debt.)

The cost of capital is also called the weighted-average cost of capital or WACC because the capital structure established by a company generally includes a mix of long-term debt, preferred stock and common equity. When companies determine the right proportion of these elements, the resultant mix is called the target capital structure. Maximizing the value of a company requires that the company minimize its costs, including the cost of capital used to fund projects.

For those people who like to do the math, the weighted-average cost of capital in equation form is:

WACC = (Proportion of debt used * after tax cost of debt)
+ (Proportion of preferred stock used * cost of preferred stock)
+ (Proportion of common equity used * cost of common equity)

[Note: The cost of common equity can be associated with retained earnings and/or new equity.]

Gaining access to capital and acknowledging the cost of that capital is critical for making long-term investment decisions. The capital I am speaking of includes long-term debt, preferred stock and common equity (common stock and retained earnings). As a matter of good financial practice, long-term projects should always be financed with long-term funds. Companies can experience serious problems like assuming additional risk by choosing to finance long-term projects with short-term debt.

The academic translation of the above is:

$$\text{WACC} = \underset{\text{Debt}}{W_d K_d (1\text{-}T)} + \underset{\text{Preferred stock}}{W_{ps} K_{ps}} + \underset{\text{Common Equity}}{W_{ce} (K_{re} \text{ or } K_e)}$$

Where:

Appendix

| | | |
|---|---|---|
| WACC | = | Weighted-average cost of capital |
| $W_d$ | = | The proportion or weighting of debt in the total capital structure |
| $K_d$ | = | Cost of debt |
| T | = | Tax rate |
| $W_{ps}$ | = | The proportion or weighting of preferred stock in the total capital structure |
| $K_{ps}$ | = | Cost of preferred stock |
| $W_{ce}$ | = | The proportion or weighting of common equity in the total capital structure |
| $K_{re}$ | = | Cost of retained earnings |
| $K_e$ | = | Cost of new equity issued |

I will address each of these components very briefly because there should be a group in your company (such as the finance or treasury department) that is responsible for calculating the WACC. Because of the complexity, project managers should not attempt to calculate their own WACC. Let an experienced professional assist you. Please consult a graduate or undergraduate level textbook on financial management if you desire more information on the theoretical derivation of the WACC. This higher-level review of the components of the WACC should give you a good appreciation for the complexities of the evaluation.

## COST OF DEBT

Because debt produces a fixed obligation on the borrower, one would expect that determining its cost would be rather straightforward. It usually does not pose a problem for the financial analysts trained in working with the various forms of debt instruments, but this topic is quite complex for the uninformed or casual user. Some of the variables considered in determining the cost of debt include:

✧ Incorporating the cost of any short-term debt if it is used (in addition to long-term debt and despite the recommendation not to use it) as part of the strategy for financing capital projects

✧ Accounting for any debt with floating interest rates, sinking funds or convertible features

✧ Accounting for the cost of issuing the debt (i.e. investment banker and legal fees)

Each of these complexities affects the cost of debt. Your financial analyst knows the form of debt that is typically used in your company and is in a much better position to determine its cost.

A final word of caution: you must exercise great care in selecting the tax rate for calculating the after-tax cost of debt. Be sure the tax rate that you (or your financial analyst) are using in your WACC calculation is consistent with the tax rate assumption used in the financial analysis section. Using inconsistent assumptions is a very easy trap to fall into since different groups typically prepare the project assumptions and WACC calculations. Documenting and communicating all assumptions and getting the experts involved will prevent any inconsistencies in your analysis.

## COST OF PREFERRED STOCK

Many companies include preferred stock as part of their financing strategy. Similar to debt, preferred stock implies a fixed obligation to pay. It is not mandatory that companies pay preferred stock dividends, but failing to do so could have serious repercussions. These repercussions could include experiencing difficulty raising additional capital or much worse, losing control of the firm. Companies consider these obligations fixed because the consequences of not complying are usually severe.

And like debt, calculating the cost of preferred stock is equally challenging because there are many variations. Some preferred stock has call features and sinking funds for example. One big difference between preferred stock and debt is the tax benefits available to the firm. Whereas the interest payments on debt are tax deductible, preferred stock dividends are not. The company must bear the full cost. As a result, preferred stock is more costly to the company than debt.

## COST OF EQUITY

Companies acquire equity by either retaining their earnings (net income after taxes and preferred stock dividends) or by issuing new common stock. Although retained earnings comes from the operations of the business and seem free, there is definitely an opportunity cost to the investor. The shareholder always has the option of taking those retained earnings out of the company as dividends and reinvesting them somewhere else. Shareholders would be indifferent whether the company retains their earnings or pays them out as dividends if the company earns a return on par with similar investments of like risk. The shareholder can demand two things of management if the business is not providing adequate financial returns:

1. Either pay out 100% of the earnings (after taxes and preferred stock dividends) as common stock dividends or stock repurchases so their funds can be reinvested elsewhere

2. Improve the operational performance of the company so that it generates an acceptable return on investment

Common stockholders demand more from the company and expect to earn a higher rate of return on their investment than debt holders and preferred stockholders. Common stockholders are more demanding because they bear the risk of being the last one in line should the company face trouble and by forced to liquidate.

Calculating the cost of a company's retained earnings (or the rate of return expected by shareholders) is quite difficult and should be the responsibility of your finance department. Three methods for calculating the cost are commonly used:

1. The capital asset pricing model
2. The discounted cash flow method
3. The risk-adjusted bond yield method

This book will not examine these different theoretical approaches. Please refer to other financial management texts if you desire more detailed information.

After exhausting its supply of retained earnings, the company must then turn to issuing new common stock if it still needs additional funding for its capital programs. This is a very common occurrence for companies experiencing rapid growth. One frequently sees private, high-growth companies filing initial public offerings or IPOs as a means of gaining access to greater funding sources. Newly issued common stock is always more costly than retained earnings because the company must incur additional charges to issue the common stock. These additional charges are for the investment banker and lawyer fees associated with placing the issue in the marketplace.

In summary, the four components of the cost of capital are rank ordered according to their cost to the company:

## Most Costly

Equity – new common stock

Equity – retained earnings

Preferred stock

Debt

## Least Costly

## OTHER CONSIDERATIONS – FINANCIAL DISTRESS

One might suggest that the company use mostly debt to finance its capital programs because it is cheaper. This is true to a point, but you must exercise great caution. Companies that have too much debt on the balance sheet run the risk of incurring financial distress. If the company faces hard times, it may find itself at a competitive disadvantage because it is saddled with debt repayments and interest charges. The lack of readily accessible funding may result in missed opportunities or weakened defensive capabilities. Finding the proper mix of debt, preferred stock and equity (the target capital structure) for your company is very difficult, and an inaccurate calculation in this area can easily negate all the good work accomplished in building your cost and benefit assumptions.

Appendix

## ADJUSTING FOR RISK

The WACC, as determined for the company's target capital structure, is primarily designed for projects of average risk. We all know, however, that not all projects are created equal. A project for developing a new, unproven product line is inherently more risky than a project for upgrading a computer system with proven technology. Should these projects be evaluated using the same WACC? Similarly, should a company with multiple divisions or subsidiaries use one common WACC or should it develop unique WACCs for each area?

Ideally, different WACCs should be used for different levels of risk because shareholders demand higher rates of return on investments that are subject to greater risk. Calculating these risk adjustments on a project-by-project basis is quite difficult in practice, and companies usually end up classifying their projects subjectively by adjusting their WACC up or down accordingly. Other companies will develop a WACC that is specific to a division or business unit. This can be fairly easy to do if there are standalone competitors to use as reference points. Finding a comparable set of financial information on any particular line of business is difficult in practice because most publicly reported companies are usually in more than one line of business. They often manage a very diverse portfolio of products and services. Despite the difficulty in obtaining benchmark data, the uniqueness of each division's projects would argue for using division-specific WACCs. But how many companies actually follow the preferred theoretical approach?

Many large conglomerates still use a single WACC for project analysis regardless of the differences in their businesses or risk of their projects. The biggest benefit of using only one WACC is simplicity because one measure is far easier to manage and communicate. These companies have reasoned that designing overly complex analytical rules and processes loses more value. The overhead needed to interpret the rules and enforce compliance outweighs the benefits of greater precision in their opinion.

Your company must decide for itself whether the "one-size-fits-all" approach is appropriate or whether division-specific hurdle rates are better. Have your finance department take responsibility for making this decision. Unless there are no other available resources, do not attempt to calculate the cost of capital yourself. Insist that your finance department prepare and communicate the appropriate WACC estimates for use in your business cases.

Managing the company's sources of funds, whether it is debt, preferred stock or common equity, is a very complex function—which is why most people are oblivious to the costs associated with financing a company. To them, the cost of capital is simply a number that some finance guy gives to you. As project managers or sponsors seeking access to the company's funds, it is important to have a good understanding of the costs associated with that funding.

The cost of capital is the measuring stick that management uses to help determine who gets access to the company's funds.

# INDEX

Index

## ABOUT THE AUTHOR

Patrick Gregory is a graduate of the University of Michigan and the Harvard Business School. He has extensive experience within the automotive, aerospace, financial services and utility industries. Pat has successfully managed major cost reduction programs as well as redesigned the budgeting, forecasting and strategic planning processes at several companies. He also has extensive experience with financial systems and improving the financial reporting process. He has taught financial management at the Executive MBA level and has a gift for making the complex easy to understand.

Pat is co-founder of Living Spirit Press and founder and President of the Stonehaven Group, a financial management-consulting firm that helps companies achieve greater efficiency and effectiveness in their financial management practices.

You can visit his website at www.maximumreturn.net, or contact him directly at patrickgregory@maximumreturn.net.

MAXIMUM RETURN
WINNER
BENJAMIN FRANKLIN AWARD
BEST BUSINESS BOOK

To obtain additional copies of this book or information on other
Maximum Return products, please visit our website at:
www.maximumreturn.net